Documents on
Contemporary Crafts

No. 3

Crafting Exhibitions

André Gali (ed.)

NORWEGIAN CRAFTS
2015

Table of Contents

Acknowledgements

One of the most common places for the public to encounter works of craft is in an exhibition, be it in a museum, a gallery, a fair or somewhere else. For Norwegian Crafts, producing exhibitions is one way to strengthen the position of contemporary craft and to facilitate various types of exchange between Norwegian and international craft and design. While working on producing exhibitions, sometimes also curating them, Norwegian Crafts has experienced a need to focus critically on the exhibition as a medium, to explore various forms of exhibition making and to discuss it as an act not just of administration, but also of creativity.

Norwegian Crafts is therefore proud to present *Crafting Exhibitions*, a book that aims to stimulate critical thinking about curating and exhibition design within the field of contemporary craft. This is also the third volume in the series *Documents on Contemporary Crafts*. The first book, *Museum for Skills*, was published in 2013, and the second book, *Materiality Matters*, was published in 2014. They both quickly became popular and sought-after publications amongst craft students and professionals internationally. For this present book, we are happy to be collaborating with Arnoldsche Art Publishers, a publishing company with expertise on books in the field of crafts and with an extensive international distribution network.

Norwegian Crafts is thankful for the enthusiasm and interest from Arnoldsche's editors Dirk Allgaier and Marion Boschka. We are also deeply thankful for the support received from Norway's Ministry of Foreign Affairs and Arts Council Norway; without their generous financial aid, this publication would not have been possible. We extend a final and special thanks to André Gali for his work with this third edition of the series.

Trude G. Ugelstad
Executive Director, Norwegian Crafts

Preface

The craft of exhibition making has become increasingly interesting to me over the years. Working as an art critic and as editor for *Norwegian Crafts Magazine*[1] and *KUNSTforum*,[2] it has been my privilege to review a great number of exhibitions, biennales and fairs, and to interview a variety of artists, curators, museum directors and gallery owners. Seeing exhibitions and learning about how curators work and think have been inspirational for my own thinking about art, the exhibition as a medium, and about how contexts and critical discourses influence the viewer's experience.

Two of the curators I've had the pleasure to talk with are Glenn Adamson,[3] now director at the Museum of Art and Design (MAD) in New York, and Maria Lind,[4] director of Tensta Konsthall in Stockholm. With Adamson I discussed different ways of curating and thinking about crafts, from an encyclopedic survey-approach to a more intimate, personal approach. From Lind I learned about curating as a way of criticizing the art institution, about curatorial models that challenge the structures of time and space commonly deployed in art institutions, and about art as a prototype for social models. I am very glad that they both agreed to share some of their curatorial experiences in this book.

I have also learned a lot from the two other contributors. Anne Britt Ylvisåker, senior curator at KODE – Art Museums of Bergen, is an important curator and thinker within the 'traditional' museum context, and has lectured at several seminars I've attended over the years. Her research on collecting artworks that may not be easily preserved shows how the works themselves can challenge the notion of

---

1 *Norwegian Crafts Magazine* is an online publication with 4 to 5 issues per year. I have been the editor-in-chief for this magazine since 2010. www.norwegiancrafts.no

2 *KUNSTforum* is a Nordic art quarterly that I founded with Tore Næss and Nicolai Strøm-Olsen in 2009, and which I have edited since. www.kunstforum.as

3 *Norwegian Crafts Magazine* issue 02/ 2013: *What's Important about Craft?*

4 *KUNSTforum* 4/ 2011: *Institusjonskritikeren som vil utfordre kunsten [The Institutonal Critic that Aims to Challenge Art]*.

conserving versus representation, which in turn leads to discussions about the degree to which the museum staff become the artists' collaborative partners.

Last but not least, Marianne Zamecznik, a free-lance curator and exhibition designer, is at the forefront of thinking about curatorial models and exhibition design. She has invented curatorial approaches for crafts and material-based practices that emphasize the exhibition as a dynamic process which begins well in advance of the actual, physical exhibition. Through open-ended curatorial concepts, she reimagines the selection process and what an exhibition may be.

These four curators offer very different approaches to the craft of exhibition making, showing some of the possibilities and challenges of working with the medium of the exhibition. I hope this book will give readers an understanding of some of the processes that go into making an exhibition, from developing concepts to the physical realization. By showing different modes of working with exhibiting, I hope the book can contribute to a rethinking and revitalization of the exhibition format within the field of crafts.

André Gali
Editor

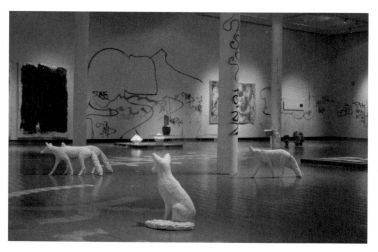

Installation view, *Crafts 2014* at KODE – Art Museums in Bergen. In front:
Therese Hoen: *I've read that too much traveling is a waste of time*, 2013/14, in
middle from left to right: Ingjerd Mandt: *Terrin* I & II, 2014, Sofia Koryfilis: *Bare
bøy*, 2014, Magrete Loe Elde: *Tøy* I, II & III, 2014, in back from left to right: Hanne
Øverland: *Under-Inni*, 2014, Kirsten Opem: *Uten tittel*, 2013, Gitte Magnus:
Biedermeier- og polkagriser, 2014. Exhibition design: Morten & Jonas.
Photo: André Gali

New Modes of Curating and Presenting Craft

An introduction to the craft of exhibition making

André Gali

*The leading questions [in many discussions on contemporary art]
have been how ideas are manifested spatially, negotiated contextually
and mediated publicly.*[1]

In this introduction I look at the role of the curator, exploring it first
by examining an exhibition curated by Harald Szeemann. This is followed up with a deeper look into four exhibitions from 2014, each of
which says something about the balance between the artworks and
their context. The exhibitions are *Crafts 2014* at KODE – Art Museums
of Bergen, *Martino Gamper: Design Is a State of Mind* at the Serpentine
Gallery in London, *BACK! Everything Must Go!* at Rösskha Museum in
Gothenburg, and last year's master´s degree exhibition at the Arts and
Crafts Department at Oslo Academy of the Arts. This last exhibition
was curated by Marianne Zamecznik, who will reflect further on it in
her essay in this book. Finally, I will try to draw some conclusions about
these shows and convey why I perceive them as interesting examples
when discussing new modes of curating and presenting crafts to the
public. Three of these exhibitions took place within the framework
of museums, while the master´s degree show and *Design Is a State of
Mind* were held in 'white cubes'. I will not discuss the ideology of the
museum and the white cube (although these are interesting discussions in their own right), but rather focus on the exhibitions themselves. I must stress that I'm an art critic with no practical experience
in curating, so the views I present here are based on my own experience
of exhibitions and my subsequent critical reflection.

---

1   Sofia Hernandez Chong Cuy: What About Collecting?, in Jens Hoffmann (ed.)
    Ten Fundamental Questions of Curating, Milan: Mousse Publishing, 2013, p. 58.

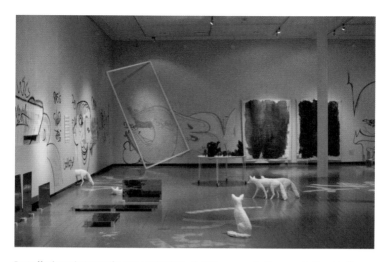

Installation view, *Crafts 2014* at KODE – Art Museums in Bergen. In front left to right: Iulian Bulai: *Feetfulness,* 2012, Therese Hoen: *I've read that too much traveling is a waste of time*, 2013/14, in middle: Jim Darbu: *First Contact*, 2013, in back from left to right: Tora Endestad Bjørkheim: *Proposal*, 2013, Hanne Øverland: *Under-Inni*, 2014, & *Grunnstoff*, 2012-2014. Exhibition design: Morten & Jonas. Photo: André Gali

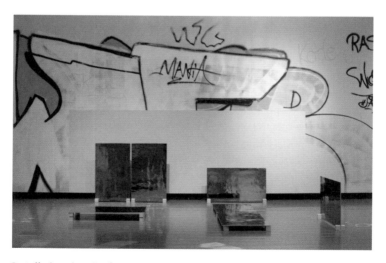

Installation view, *Crafts 2014* at KODE – Art Museums in Bergen. Iulian Bulai: *Feetfulness*, 2012. Exhibition design: Morten & Jonas. Photo: André Gali

Curatorial discourse has been an increasingly important aspect of contemporary art for more than 50 years. In the 1960s the German term *Ausstellungsmacher* and the French *faiseur d'expositions* were introduced into the critical language surrounding the institution of art. According to Paul O'Neill, these terms served to emphasize the emerging role of the *freelance curator* as a maker of large-scale, independent group exhibitions outside the museum structure.[2] With this, it seems like a new mode of thinking about exhibitions emerged, and that the curator took on a new role as an 'author' of exhibitions. Renowned curators from the early days of curatorial discourse were Harald Szeemann, Walter Hopps, Pontus Hultén and Seth Siegelaub. With these independent exhibition makers, each with his own particular curatorial signature, the 'exhibition form' was reflected on and 'treated as a medium in and of itself'.[3]

Szeemann's exhibition *Live in Your Head: When Attitudes Become Form (Works – Concepts – Processes – Situations – Information)* at Kunsthalle Bern in 1969, can serve as an example of this new role for the curator. The exhibition is famous within the field of curatorial discourse, so much so that it was reconstructed in Fondazione Prada at Ca' Corner della Regina, Venice, in 2013.[4] Here a great number of artworks were grouped together to serve a narrative that Szeemann had conceptualized, making the works appear as sharing artistic interests and concerns and thus belonging to an art historical tendency. In the case of *When Attitudes Become Form*, rather than just selecting existing works, the artists were asked to make works especially for the exhibition, sometimes creating them in the actual exhibition space (this curatorial structure was also used in several other exhibitions at the time).

When talking about exhibitions, it is urgent to understand what an exhibition is. The word 'exhibition' has roots in legal terminology – the display of evidence in a court of law. The evidence can consist of documents or some sort of physical object, for instance a weapon, used

2   Paul O'Neill: The Culture of Curating and the Curating of Culture, London: MIT Press, 2012, p. 14.

3   Ibid, p. 16.

4   http://www.myartguides.com/venice-art-biennale-2013/exhibitions/item/608-when-attitudes-become-form-bern-1969-venice-2013 (visited 13 February 2015)

to try to prove that a defendant is guilty or not guilty of the crime of which he or she is accused. The exhibited evidence is provided for the jury to inspect and evaluate, and it can either strengthen or weaken the defendant's defence. Turning to art exhibitions; the exhibited works serve as evidence of an overall narrative. An important aspect, in my opinion, is the jury who evaluate the objects, and in the context of an art exhibition, the jury could consist of art critics and/or the public. The exhibition can be perceived as the medium through which works of art become meaningful. And it has to do with presenting them to the public.

Before the curator emerged as an independent agent introducing an individual narrative, the narrative in an exhibition (of whatever sort) was presented as an authoritative truth. This is still the case in many museums today. The emergence of the freelance curator or 'curator as free agent' thus implies that there are no absolute truths about art, or the world, and that there can only be suggestions. We could also say that new truths are produced through curating. As Mary Anne Staniszewski puts it, 'selecting what is included and excluded is one way in which culture is produced'.[5] The exhibition is thus a medium that constantly produces new cultural narratives.

At any rate, the exhibition is not a *neutral* medium, as Elena Filipovic points out. She describes how the exhibition has served different ideological positions, as 'a machine for the manufacture of meaning, a theatre of bourgeois culture, a site for disciplining of citizen-subjects, or a mise-en-scène of unquestioned values (linear time, teleological history, master narratives)'.[6] Many of today's curatorial strategies question the idea of a master narrative, thus presenting the exhibition medium as a discursive statement in an ongoing history of exhibitions.

Neutrality
The question of whether or not the exhibition is a neutral medium came to the fore last autumn in connection with *Craft 2014*, an annual, juried exhibition administrated by the Norwegian Association for Art

5   Paul O'Neill: The Culture of Curating and the Curating of Culture, London: MIT Press, 2012, p. 40.
6   Elena Filipovic: What is an Exhibition? in Ten Fundamental Questions of Curating (ed. Jens Hoffmann), Milan: Mousse Publishing, Fiorucci Art Trust, 2013, p. 74-75.

and Crafts. The exhibition was held at KODE – Art Museums of Bergen, and gained distinction through fostering a debate on the relationship between exhibition design and artworks. The exhibition room was covered in tagging made by local graffiti artists. This was the idea of the exhibition designer, since the annual show is not curated. Most critics despised *Craft 2014*, arguing that the works had to fight with the exhibition design for viewers' attention; they missed the experience of good artworks due to the tagging's brutal expression.

Øystein Hauge, art critic in the leading local newspaper, *Bergens Tidende*, wrote in his review that 'This frame is in danger of making everything we see seem stupid'.[7]

Art critic Sigrun Hodne, writing for the national weekly *Morgenbladet*, followed Hauge in his antipathy towards the exhibition design, underscoring that most of the works were great, had they not been forced to do battle with such a terrible visual environment. In her review 'Craft in Battle', she wrote: 'I will go as far as to say that the exhibition design is mocking the artist'.[8]

As sort of a closure to the controversy, art critic Erlend Hammer wrote in his review 'Design Boost' in *Kunsthåndverk* 4/ 2014, that it is impossible to overlook the fact that 'the exhibition is characterized by what can be called a confrontational, interventional curatorial model.[9]

Hammer, like many others, read the exhibition design as the choice of a curator. It was not, but that fact may not have made much difference since many artists, critics and curators seem to expect, and anticipate, that craft exhibitions should put the works in the centre of attention and downplay the surroundings. This seems to be a general way of perceiving crafts exhibitions; craft objects should either be presented in the (supposedly neutral) white cube, or, following the logic of the decorative art museum, in glass vitrines and on plinths. These two dominant modes of curating and presenting crafts are rarely challenged by spectacular exhibitions or signature-curators. In my opinion, the exhibition of craft suffers from the idea that there is (and should be) no curation, or that there is a particular way of curating and displaying that is almost neutral. Objects are displayed as singular

---

7 Øystein Hauge: Kunsthåndverkets uutholdelige letthet, Bergens Tidende 19 October 2014.

8 Sigrun Hodne: Kunsthåndverk i kamp, Morgenbladet 17 October 2014.

9 Erlend Hammer: Designløftet, Kunsthåndverk 4/ 2014.

phenomena with little or no relation to other objects. Only to a minor degree is the exhibition discussed as an 'object' in its own right. Nor is there much discussion about the exhibition as medium, how it communicates or what it does.

As Elene Filipovic puts it, 'an exhibition isn't only the sum of its artworks, but also the relationships created between them, the dramaturgy around them, and the discourse that frames them'.[10]

Exhibition as medium

If *Craft 2014* was defined by its opposition between objects and exhibition design, Martino Gamper's exhibition at the Serpentine Sackler Gallery in London, *Design Is a State of Mind,* was defined by its holistic quality. It worked on many levels, and there was fruitful interplay between the details and the show as a whole.

What Gamper did, as he told *Wallpaper,*[11] was simply to show 'interesting things collected by interesting people on interesting shelves'. He selected many different shelves, many of them one-offs, from designers such as Franco Albini, Ettore Sottsass, Ponti, Andrea Branzi, Michele De Lucchi and Vico Magistretti, Charlotte Perriand, Alvar Aalto for Artek, Vitsoe and Ercol. He also included some of his own shelves and a few from Ikea. On the shelves he put collections of objects borrowed from 'friends, friends of friends, tutors and students' – people who Gamper knew were 'inveterate hoarders of inspirational objects'.[12]

His efforts resulted is an amazing aesthetic experience of each collection of objects. The exhibition showed a designer's sensibility for display, and this is something that is often lacking in exhibitions of fine art and crafts. Gamper caused the exhibition itself to become a work of art – or maybe we should say craft, since it was 'crafted' so well. It was personal. It had a kind of narrative structure the audience could walk through – from shelf to shelf, from collection to collection. The shelves

---

10 Elena Filipovic: What is an Exhibition? in Ten Fundamental Questions of Curating (ed. Jens Hoffmann), Milan: Mousse Publishing, Fiorucci Art Trust, 2013, p. 75.

11 http://www.wallpaper.com/design/martino-gamper-design-is-a-state-of-mind-at-the-serpentine-sackler-gallery-in-london/7231#5Gds1hGLUz0DIOcR.99 (visited 13 January 2015)

12 Ibid.

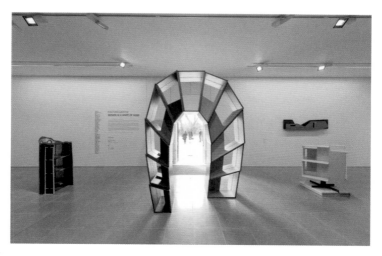

Martino Gamper
Installation view, *design is a state of mind*

Left to right:
Gaetano Pesce: *Nobody's Shelves Short Body* 2002, Coloured polyurethane resin.
Courtesy of Nilufar Gallery
Martino Gamper: *L'Arco della Pace* 2009, Coloured veneer, poplar plywood.
Courtesy of Martino Gamper. Co-produced by Museion, Bolzano, Italy and
Pinacoteca Giovanni e Marella Agnelli, Turin, Italy
Giò Ponti: *Altamira* 1950-1953, Oak. Courtesy of Nilufar Gallery
Claudio Salocchi: *Bookcase* 1960, Metal, lacquered wood. Courtesy of
Nilufar Gallery
Photograph: © 2014 Hugo Glendinning

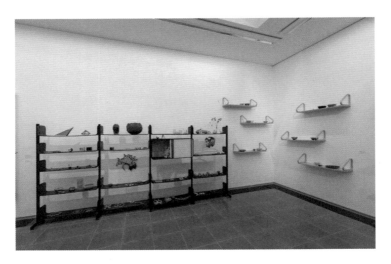

Martino Gamper
Installation view, *design is a state of mind*

Left to right:
Campo Graffi: *Bookcase* 1950s, Rosewood, metal. Courtesy of Nilufar Gallery.
Objects courtesy of Bethan Wood
Alvar Aalto: *112B Wall Shelf* 1936 / 1960's, Birch veneer, natural lacquer. Courtesy
of Artek. Objects courtesy of Fabien Capello
Photograph: © 2014 Hugo Glendinning

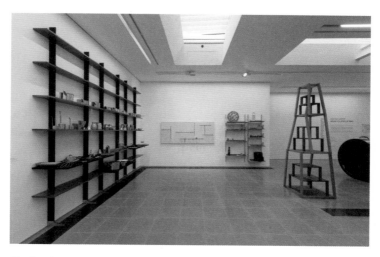

Martino Gamper
Installation view, *design is a state of mind*

Left to right:
Ignazio Gardella: *Bookcase* 1970, Wood, black lacquered metal. Courtesy of
Nilufar Gallery. Objects courtesy of Mats Theselius
Andrea Branzi: *Wall bookshelf* 2011, Toulipiè, crystal. Courtesy of Nilufar Gallery.
Objects courtesy of Daniel Eatock
Osvaldo Borsani: *L 60* 1946, Metal, teak. Courtesy of Nilufar Gallery. Objects
courtesy of Rupert Blanchard
Michele De Lucchi: *Montefeltro* 2008, Oak frame, walnut elements, linseed oil.
Courtesy of Nilufar Gallery
Photograph: © 2014 Hugo Glendinning

were interesting in themselves as aesthetically designed objects, and also with regard to the concept of colleting, but they were only really fulfilled by the items placed upon them. The way the shelves were organized in relation to each other offered multiple ways of moving about the exhibition.

Context is everything

A display need not have static surroundings or be the end product of a curatorial process. It can also involve various modes of interaction with the public. This point was proven by the exhibition *BACK. Everything Must Go!* at Röhsska Museum in Gothenburg last year. The exhibition was created specifically for the museum by fashion designer Ann-Sofie Back, in connection with her winning the prestigious Torsten and Wanja Söderberg Prize. Normally the winners of this prize show a retrospective presentation of their works, but Back seized the opportunity to make the 'shop of her dreams' [13] – a conceptual store with a range of products specially made for the exhibition and closely linked to several of the clothing collections she had designed over the years. These products, which were for sale during the exhibition, where displayed in a kind of variety store setting using aesthetics and colours usually associated with cheapness.

Characteristic for Back's exhibition display was the use of posters with catch phrases like 'Everything must go' and 'Only 99 kr', etc. The products, from soap and condoms to sunglasses and thongs, were exhibited alongside examples of key garments from some of Back's collections. The whole store was framed by a see-through metal grid structure that differentiated Back's exhibition space from the rest of the museum.

The store's cheap look, which was reinforced by the display and promotion of products as bargains, stood in contrast to the fashion logic linked with brand names (in this case *Back*), and with the cultural logic that treats the museum as a space for high culture. Conceptually then, Back's exhibition challenged two notions of display: the fashion display we expect to see in luxury stores and on the cat walk, and the type of display we expect to see in museums. Through juxtaposing sign systems, this exhibition undermined conventions

---

13 http://rohsska.se/utstallningar/tidigare/7648/ (last visited 11 February 2015)

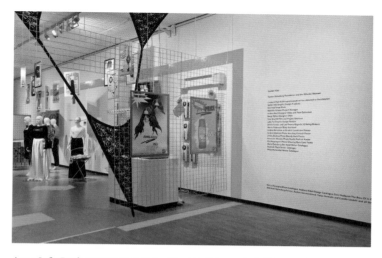

Anne Sofie Back: BACK! Everything Must Go! Photo: Carl Oliver Ander, Röhsska museet

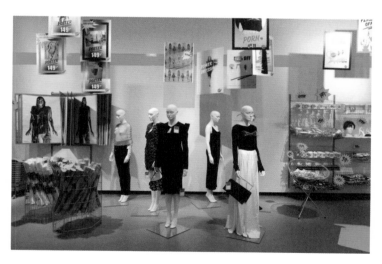

Anne Sofie Back: BACK! Everything Must Go! Photo: Carl Oliver Ander, Röhsska museet

of display and emphasized how the framing of a product – as soap, fashion or a work of art – is significant for the cultural and economic value of that product.

Thinking about how to present art to the public

A somewhat unusual exhibition that has challenged the notion of exhibition making and put the exhibition medium in the spotlight was the 2014 show for students earning a 'Master of Visual Art' degree at Oslo National Academy of the Arts (KHiO). The title for this exhibition was a sentence borrowed from Michel Foucault's book *The Order of Things: An Archaeology of the Human Sciences*. Foucault refers to a text by Jorge Luis Borges that challenges the notion of taxonomy. (As I understand it, it was meant as an analogy for discussions within the craft field, on how to define what one is doing):

[A] 'certain Chinese encyclopedia' in which it is written that 'animals are divided into: (a) belonging to the Emperor, (b) embalmed, (c) tame, (d) sucking pigs, (e) sirens, (f) fabulous, (g) stray dogs, (h) included in the present classification, (i) frenzied, (j) innumerable, (k) drawn with a very fine camelhair brush, (l) et cetera, (m) having just broken the water pitcher, (n) that from a long way off look like flies'.[14]

At the beginning of the 2013/14 school year, freelance curator Marianne Zamecznik – hired by KHiO to curate the graduation show for Master students in what was then known as the Visual Arts department[15] – asked the students to imagine what their most apt graduation show would look like: what would serve their project best in terms of display? She then asked them to realize that show. Each student made his or her individual project during the course of the school year and had the option of either creating a model for how to exhibit it and facilitate the public's experience of it, or to follow through and present the actual work to the public. The students did not need to do a white cube exhibition, and several chose particular venues for presenting their projects. One student presented a battle rap at the avant-garde jazz bar Blå, another collaborated with a church, asking the priest to discuss

---

14 Michel Foucault: The Order of Things: An Archaeology of the Human Sciences, London: Routledge, 1970, p. xv.

15 The department changed its name to 'Art and Craft' in autumn 2014.

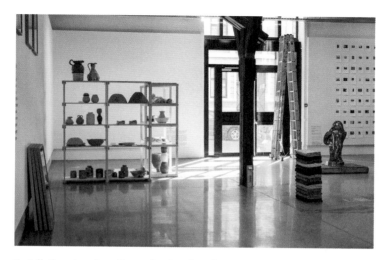

Installation view, from the graduation show for Master Degree students at Oslo National Academy of the Arts (KHiO) 2014, curated by Marianne Zamecznik. Left to right: Victoria Günzler: *Samtidsarkeologi*, 2014, Julia Gvein Andresens: *Stay Level*, 2014, Iulian Bulai: *Working like a Chinese worker* (part of a larger project), 2014. Photo: André Gali

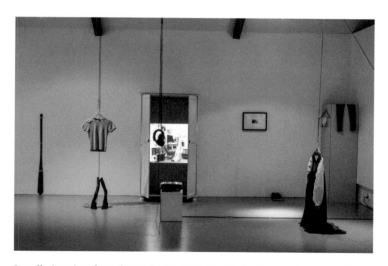

Installation view, from the graduation show for Master Degree students at Oslo National Academy of the Arts (KHiO) 2014, curated by Marianne Zamecznik. Signe Arnborg Løvaas' graduate works. Photo: André Gali

her works in a sermon. A third chose to curate two shows – one in her vacated apartment, the other in a designer shop. And so on.

In this way, the students were forced to think not only about creating their work, but about display, presentation, venue and how to enable the public to experience it. This approach activated the idea that a work of art first becomes so when it is exhibited or presented to an audience.

Exhibition as avatar

When the students' degree show finally opened in KHiO's own gallery space in June 2014, what was on display was not the original projects, but a sort of retelling of the projects they had created during the school year. These retellings or representations Zamecznik called 'avatars'.

The word avatar is perhaps best known from the Hollywood movie *Avatar* (2009). In it, a human soldier goes to another planet and assumes the shape of an alien being as a means to infiltrate that species. Although the word has lately been used to refer to a virtual world – meaning a virtual representation of a real person – this stands in contrast to the word's more originary meaning. In Sanskrit, an *avatāra* is a manifestation of a Hindu deity who has descended to earth, becoming incarnate in either human or animal form.

The exhibition seemed to correspond to both meanings: as a concept that comes to life or is materialized (parallel to the deity becoming earthly), and as a reality that becomes conceptual / virtual through its representation. Regardless of how one chooses to interpret the concept of the avatar, the exhibition addressed complex questions about representation, display and the taxonomy of contemporary craft.

Conclusion

The exhibitions I have mentioned here raise questions about important aspects of exhibition making. In its desire to reinvent the exhibition space, *Craft 2014* challenged the balance between the artworks and the framing narrative created by the exhibition design, creating a fictional space for these objects and thus partaking in a larger discourse on the relationship between artists' intentions and the exhibition concept. The exhibition's novelty lay in the disregard of conventional display, and in the combination of signs of modern urbanity – the tagging and graffiti – and the crafted objects. It raised questions about the museum space as a neutral and natural habitat for craft objects. After all, craft often belongs to a tradition of utility that is downplayed in museum exhibitions. To elucidate, a question often raised in connection with jewellery exhibitions is whether art jewellery should be presented as sculptural objects or as wearable design items.

While the novelty in *Craft 2014* had to do with the presentation of objects, Gamper's exhibition at Serpentine did not question presentation as much as it seamlessly combined design and objects from various contexts into a narrative about collecting and the display of identity. Its success may have come from the fact that the curator was himself a designer who focused on the value system of design. In his exhibition, instead of emphasizing differences between the actual objects, he managed to present the exhibition as a sensuous experience of composition and form.

As for *BACK! Everything Must Go!*, the exhibition played with concepts of consumption, experience and the value systems of art and fashion. Not content with just showing her collections, Back treated the experience of buying as part of the core of her exhibition, and in doing so, made other consumer products available for museum visitors. The objects in this context took on a dual identity, as souvenirs like those we might find in a museum shop, or as products merely to be used. By surrounding the objects with an ironic design aesthetic imitating cheap variety shops, this duality was heightened and placed centre stage. Thus Back revealed both the logic of the fashion brand name and the logic of the artwork, undermining the idea of luxury value that is associated with fashion and the idea of the artwork as high culture.

Finally, Marianne Zamecznik's 'avatar'-exhibition dealt with the exhibition format on many levels, introducing a productive discourse into the critical language surrounding the institution of crafts. I think this exhibition can teach us something important about the relationship between objects and their context, and serve as a starting point for exploring new modes of curating and presenting crafts.

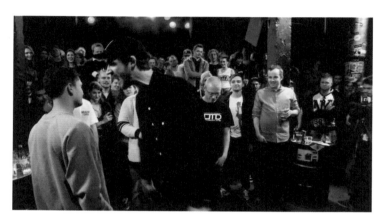

André Jarnvig Jensen battlerrap vs Dobbel (Sindre Stordal) at Blå in Oslo, 22.02.2014.

Exhibition Making as a Driving Force in Contemporary Craft Discourse

Marianne Zamecznik

My experience and engagement with contemporary craft comes from studying at the Department of Art and Craft at Oslo National Academy of Arts, and from working as a guest lecturer at the school. I've made exhibitions with works that could be labelled contemporary art or craft, but the distinction between the two is neither important nor clear to me. My position from the outset is that I don't think the field of craft needs a separate set of theories and display strategies to cater to its needs. This is because many relevant theories already exist, and more are developing at a high pace in the field of contemporary art; these theories and strategies can be applied to contemporary craft. The field of craft cannot match the speed at which discourses are developing in contemporary art, simply because there are too few theoreticians, writers, historians and curators who specialize in or work with contemporary craft. Practitioners in this field can easily borrow, hack and over-write theory from other fields to underpin what's happening in the field of craft today. These adaptations can happen on many levels, be it artistic, theoretical, institutional or political, and in the following I will argue that original exhibitions and innovative modes of display are crucial for driving the discourses in contemporary craft forward.

In the text I discuss some of the relevant theories that could easily be developed in the field of contemporary craft. I consider how modes of presentation that uphold certain modes of usership can have an effect on works made by contemporary artists, and the implications this has for exhibiting and disseminating contemporary craft. I will discuss the nature and potential of objects made by artists by gleaning ideas from other vocabularies: the idea of the 'dynamic object' is from the field of conservation, and the 'flickering object' is discussed in relation to object-oriented ontology. By reconsidering the status of an object in terms of its presentation and, by extension, its use, we can start to look at how craft can take on more radical modes of display, thus advancing current and emerging discourses essential to contemporary craft.

What is an exhibition?

Having tutored master students at the Department of Art and Craft several years, I have been struck by the difficulty, for many, to relate to relevant discourses in art; they tend to have a significantly lower level of theoretical understanding than students at art academies. Artist and teacher Ernesto Pujol states that 'Students should (...) learn how to justify that creation intellectually, beyond the subjective, in our visually dense and materially cluttered world. If they don't want to do this, they have no business being professional contemporary artists'.[1] I couldn't agree more. To obtain that goal, it's my belief that one key factor is to teach students about dissemination and ways of presenting their work. Many students assume that to present their work in an exhibition involves a prearranged format that first and foremost is instrumental in reaching an audience and building a CV, which in turn leads to scholarships and other opportunities. They seldom begin by asking 'what is an exhibition?' or by considering the dissemination of their work as a thing in itself, apart from the work. It's tricky to teach master students about dissemination at a school whose traditions have strong ties to the conservative ideology of the Arts and Crafts movement of John Ruskin and William Morris, and the avant-garde traditions of the Bauhaus school. Today, the Department of Art and Craft at The National Academy of Art in Oslo is situated somewhere in-between that of Bauhaus and the modern art academy.

The Bauhaus school dismantled distinctions between fine art and craft and placed intellectual and artistic pursuits on the same level as the acquisition of manual skills. Workshop instruction and theoretical instruction were combined in order to produce works whose form and function were unified. According to this pedagogical model, a student had the potential to become an artist if he or she were introduced to a set of guiding principles.

---

1   Ernesto Pujol: On the Ground: Practical Observations for Regenerating Art Education, in Steven Henry Madoff (ed.) *Art School: Propositions for the 21st Century*, Cambridge Mass: MIT Press, 2009, p. 5.

In the twentieth century, art educations based on the traditions of the French academies moved away from techniques and traditions, toward the possibilities offered by the medium.

> The shifts in art education throughout modernity echoed the developments in contemporary arts of its time, and represented a rupture with technique and tradition. Modernism classifies art according to medium and everything this notion entails, such as particular material, support, tools, gestures, technical procedures and conventions of specificity, its relation to and difference from other media. Medium focuses on what it has to say about itself and what it has not said yet. The definition of a painter might be 'what a painter has not done, yet'.[2]

Vivian Sky Rehberg, course director and writing tutor for the MA fine art program at Piet Zwarts Institute in Rotterdam, goes on to describe the difference between the métier or craftsmanship and the modern medium:

> The métier gets practiced, the medium gets questioned; the métier gets transmitted, the medium communicates or gets communicated; the métier gets learned, the medium gets discovered; the métier is tradition, the medium is language; the métier rests on experience, the medium relies on experimentation.[3]

If we consider the exhibition as a medium in its own right, one definition of it could be 'what an exhibition maker has not done, yet'. The exhibition could be described as a format relying on experimentation, in the same way as any medium relies on experimentation; it could be seen as a field of discovery, or be described as a language in itself. It could be considered as a format that should constantly be challenged, questioned and developed, as opposed to something all too familiar, determined by unspoken tenets.

If we consider the exhibition as a medium in its own right, one definition of it could be 'what an exhibition maker has not done, yet'. Exhibitions could be described as formats relying on experimentation, in the same way as any medium relies on experimentation; an

---

2   'Deschooling/Deskilling', lecture by Vivian Sky Rehberg, paper delivered at the seminar 'Deschooling/Deskilling & Re-public', Witte de With Center for Contemporary Art, Rotterdam, 18 October 2012.

3   Ibid.

exhibition could be seen as a field of discovery, demanding innovation. Exhibitions could be described as a language in itself. The exhibition could be considered as a format that constantly should be challenged, questioned and developed, as opposed to something all too familiar, determined by unspoken tenets.

Innovation

The modern classification of art according to medium is but one of the factors propelling the insatiable quest for innovation. Other factors are market forces and the ever-faster distribution and consumption of information through digital media.

The prominent role of exhibitions in contemporary art practices implies that they are often being challenged and questioned, and exhibition makers do feel the pressure to innovate. Some artists sense that the focus on exhibitions has taken too much attention away from artworks. Anton Vidokle's manifesto 'Art without exhibitions' reveals artists' growing scepticism towards the prominence of the exhibition (along with the curator) in the field of contemporary art:

> On a certain level I think that art is primarily a public, social thing, something that moves between people. I'm not very interested in exhibitions these days. In part, this may be caused simply by an exhaustion brought about by an over-proliferation of shows. We are living in a time of an unprecedented expansion in the amount of exhibitions of contemporary art. On a more intimate level I feel that art needs other contexts to enter the lives of people, beyond being displayed in an exhibition. This is because much of artistic practice has become largely identical with everyday life activity and objects and exhibitions today are almost an exclusive context in which something can be recognized as art, making it seem that it is actually the exhibitions that produce art. But this is not true. Art is produced by artists. As an artist, the current condition feels very alienating. So I have been trying to find other ways in which art can circulate and enter social space beyond exhibitions.[4]

When tutoring students in preparation for their degree show in 2014, they and their teachers didn't overtly express scepticism until I proposed a way of organizing the show that involved two new things: First, that each student organize his or her own degree show, paying special

---

4   Anton Vidolke presented his manifesto during a panel discussion with Ute Meta Bauer and Anselm Franke (moderator: Axel John Wieder), as part of the program 'Exhibition Making and Publics II', by Based in Berlin, 23 July 2011.

attention to two factors: a) what the artwork needs in terms of presentation and context, and b) innovation. In other words, they should focus on the ideal scenario for the presentation of their work, and they should aim to do this in new and innovative ways, not considering any practical restrictions such as budget, number of visitors, the press, the market, or even the force of gravity. Limitations are the initial problem a young artist must to deal with, and not always useful when considering what the ideal presentation of an artwork might be. The students were invited to realize their degree shows as models, but in the end only one student chose to do so. They could realise their shows wherever and whenever they wanted throughout the school year. The second thing I asked was that they make representations of their individual degree shows, and in so doing, pinpoint and express the mode of presentation that they had discovered to be the most ideal for their work. These representations, which soon were dubbed 'avatars', were to be presented in the student gallery at the end of the school year.

The goal of this exercise was to help students formulate the ideal way to present their works by finding places and contexts outside the student gallery and the school. Unsurprisingly, the 23 students found many ways to present their works, some rather remarkable. Therese Mathiesen, for instance, presented her objects in the framework of an evening mass, where the priest included his interpretation of her work in his sermon. The exercise proved the student gallery to be quite obsolete.

I also wanted to draw the students' attention to the fact that an artwork can be seen as a sort of subject – that after its creation in the artist's studio, it starts living a life of its own. 'Ask the artwork what *it* needs' was one of the slogans. Part of an artwork's life is to be included in different contexts that in turn affect its meaning and value. I wanted the students to see how they could shape that trajectory by thinking, in their early ideational stage, about how an object could be presented. I wanted them to realize that this thought process could inform all subsequent stages in a work's development – irrespective of external limitations. That an art object is created in the studio one day is easy to understand, but it may be more difficult to grasp that it then embarks on a long journey and can outlive its creator.

Dynamic objects
When an artwork outlives its creator, it becomes the problem of a conservator. I find the idea of 'the dynamic object' in the field of

conservation especially interesting when considering what happens to an artwork in the course of its lifetime. For the archaeological conservator Brian Castriota, both archaeological and contemporary objects are endowed with values and meanings that are difficult to discern and at times quite contradictory:

> The conservator approaches the object with the understanding that it is composed of a material substance, which, as a semiotic agent, communicates certain meanings and significance to culture and society. These meanings are ascribed to and communicated through the material components of an object by both its creators and subsequent users, where the supposed value and significance of these meanings contribute to the conservator's ethical imperative to preserve the object for future generations or stakeholders, our silent heirs.[5]

One factor that is impossible to control is how an artwork's immaterial integrity alters over time, and how these changes affect perceptions of meaning and value. Preservation and presentation may seem at odds at first glance, but if one considers the preservation of a work's immaterial qualities over time, ways of presenting it can certainly contribute to bringing its immaterial integrity in line with current cultural discourses. By presenting the work of art in a way that puts it in relation to culture at any given time, it can generate relevant contexts and discursive frameworks; it continues to grow and produce, constructively critiquing and regenerating itself, its relation to current discourses, other artworks, the art institution, and culture or society. Otherwise the work risks being tied to vocabularies that become obsolete, to meanings that cease to be relevant to people's lives, to theories that no longer explain who we have become as a people; it becomes unable to mirror the culture or provide alternatives to it.

A conservator can passively conserve an object by placing it in a sealed container with silica gel desiccated down to zero percent relative humidity. This means the object, without being touched, can exist in an environment that inhibits change and thus increases its longevity. However, meaning and value are extrinsic properties of an

---

5   Brian Castriota: 'Plastic Integrity: Shaping the Conservation Object'. Paper delivered at Stories and Situations: The Moderation(s) Conference. Part I – Dynamic Objecthood, Witte de With Center for Contemporary Art, Rotterdam, 5 October 2013.

object, predicated on subjective or inter-subjective determinations. Any intervention into an object's life invariably privileges certain values and meanings over others, and, by extension, certain users over others. I think this fact is largely overlooked by artists who favour the white cube; it seemingly interrupts the 'pristine signal'[6] *less* than any other form of presentation. Today's conservators understand that an object's original appearance may no longer be a realistic or even desirable goal, and that a single moment, that of the creation, doesn't speak for the entirety of the object's history. Conservators recognize that they are equally responsible for preserving the so-called 'crude signals' that are determined by users and cultures to whom an object belongs. This totality of meaning and history constitutes what conservators today call the 'conservation object', which exists and extends beyond the object's material properties. This raises questions that conservators, artists and curators must all grapple with: Are the fragmenting, cross-linking and intermingling changes and transformations that interfere with the artist's intentions (as a result of the artwork's social life), good things, or things to be avoided? How do we reconcile the agency of objects (again, their 'social life') with preserving such a variable and capricious quality as integrity? As Castriota puts it: 'Are all objects endowed with meaning inherently unstable?[...] Do objects or their meanings wish to be kept fixed, static or whole; or should we embrace change and their tendency to equilibrate, as part of their dynamic objecthood?'[7]

Usership

Speaking of the 'crude signals' determined by users of artworks; it is interesting to consider the text 'Toward a Lexicon of Usership'[8] by art critic and curator Steven Wright. Here Wright tries to establish a new vocabulary for art practices, in part because today's terminology is based on a modernist tradition of representation that renders futile any attempt to talk about art in terms of use. According to Wrigth,

---

6   This is a term used by American art historian George Kubler to describe the creator's intention.

7   Brian Castriota: Plastic Integrity.

8   Stephen Wright: 'Toward A Lexicon for Usership', originally produced as part of the exhibition *The Museum of Arte* Útil, by Tania Bruguera, Van Abbemuseum, Eindhoven, 2013-2014.

usership has come to play a key role as a producer of information, meaning and value, largely due to the rise of networked culture in the past several decades, breaking down the opposition between consumption and production. As users contribute content, knowledge, knowhow and value across all sectors of life, the question as to how they should be acknowledged becomes pressing, and single authorship becomes more difficult to define.

In terms of display, it is interesting to note that usership is characterized by its scale of operation. Modes of usership, says Wright, invariably operate on a 1:1 scale:

> They are not scaled-down models of "potentially useful things or services (the kinds of tasks and devices that might well be useful if ever they were wrested from the neutering frames of artistic autonomy and allowed traction in the real.) Though 1:1 scale initiatives make use of representation in any number of ways, they are not themselves representations of anything. The usological turn in creative practice over the past two decades or so has brought with it increasing numbers of such full-scale practices, coterminous with whatever they happen to be grappling [with]. 1:1 practices are both what they are, and propositions of what they are.[9]

The 'showing' of this kind of artistic practice is in itself redundant – as it is already being presented in the world as a full scale operation, not mimicking life, but being whatever it sets out to address or do as an activity. Of the students I worked with in 2014, Andre Jarnvig Jensen best exemplified this; for several years he had been part of the battle-rap community and had taking part in battles organized on a regular basis at the club Blå in the centre of Oslo. His master's degree project was analogous to being part of that battle rap community, and he regularly participated in battles with other local and Nordic battle rap artists. His degree show was not a re-staging, but a real battle that took place in that very environment and group he was already an established member of. The only way in which his show entered the sphere of art was by his identifying himself as an artist (and actually being hackled by other battle rappers because of it), and by presenting an account of that event as an 'avatar' – a sort of para-production – in the student gallery at the end of the year.

---

9   Ibid.

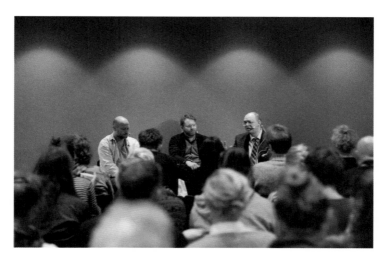

Graham Harman in conversation with Steven Claydon & Martin Clark during
Plattform at Bergen Kunsthall Saturday 10 January. Photo: Einride Torvik.

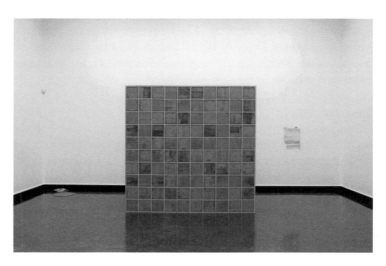

Sarah Lucas: *J1*, 2013. MDF, 100 breeze blocks, 243.5 x 243.5 x 44 cm. Numbered
edition. Courtesy Sadie Coles HQ, London. From the exhibition *The Noing Uv It*
at Bergen Kunsthall, 2015. Photo: Thor Brødreskift

Other characteristics of usership, according to Wright, are the way in which users use, borrow, steal, share, hack or alter, glean, piggyback and poach as modes of operation. He considers himself as a sort of Johnny Appleseed, spreading ideas for others to use, adapt and over-write to fit their needs (one example could be my quoting him in this text).

The idea of freely sharing ideas is something we might associate with a sort of illegal file sharing practice perpetrated by digital knights sworn to fight pay-walls and other 'evils'. Although many artists are troubled by about market forces and spend a great deal of energy talking about how art has the power to counter them, they, more often than they themselves are aware of it, tend to protect the authorship of their own work pretty fiercely. Most artists are very concerned about claiming and protecting their ideas. It trumps any other argument because it is closely related to economic conditions. Many artists feel they cannot afford to share their ideas; they therefore apply a sort of market logic as to how their ideas should be distributed and protected. As Wright points out in his text, for expert culture, use is ultimately misuse.

The relationship between artists and curators, I believe, is fragile and complicated precisely because of the question of authorship. This results in deadlock: the artwork, the idea or the object is arrested by conditions that do not allow it to operate as a thing in itself, only as an instrument to be controlled by ownership.

Speculate

The impossibility of having complete authorial control over an object is expressed in an interesting way in object-oriented ontology (OOO), a set of philosophical ideas set forth by the American philosopher Graham Harman,[10] whose work, along with that of his peers in the movement called *speculative realism* has had a strong impact on the field of aesthetics and especially art in the last few years. Challenging Kantian hegemony, speculative realism rejects the assumption of a primordial reciprocity [11] between self and world, subject and object, knower and

---

10 Object-oriented philosophy is discussed by Harman in his book *Tool-Being: Heidegger and the Metaphysics of Objects,* La Salle, Ill.: Open Court Publishing Company, 2002.

11 The mind does not simply receive information, according to Kant; it also gives that information shape.

known. The world is far weirder than we are able to even imagine. Things never conform to the ideas we have about them and does not fit into our cognitive paradigms and narrative modes of explanation. According to Harman and his colleagues, we human beings are man is not the measure of all things and this is why we must speculate; we do so in order to escape from our habitual anthropocentrism and take seriously the existence of a fundamentally alien, non-human world.

Since the launch of speculative realism at a conference at Goldsmiths College of Art in London in 2009, Graham Harman has had much traction in the field of art and architecture, much more than in the field of philosophy. One reason for this, he says, is that the field of art moves much faster than the field of philosophy, where Immanuel Kant's *Critique of Pure Reason* from 1781 is still considered a contemporary work. Harman's version of speculative realism references thinkers such as Bruno Latour and Manuel De Landa in approaching the being of things apart from us. Whereas Kant says we cannot know things in themselves because we can only experience them through our own limited understanding, Harman generalizes this to the whole cosmos, saying that none of the multitude of objects in the world, not just cognitive beings, has access to any other object (or even to itself) in more than a superficial way. According to Kant, we must not speculate about things we cannot know.[12] Harman's position is that precisely because we cannot know things in themselves, the only thing left to do is to speculate. While we cannot access objects cognitively, he argues, we can allude to them through metaphors or other aesthetic practices. In this way we can cherish things, even though we don't fully understand them. The real is something that cannot be known, only loved.[13]

In my opinion, the contemporary crafted object can do pretty well in that total rehashing of everything implied by the existence of a fundamentally alien, non-human world. The thing is there in front of us.

---

12 Kant insisted that philosophy must start with scrutinizing, and thereby accounting for, its own foundations. If it failed to do this, and instead launched directly into metaphysical speculation, then only nonsense would result. For Kant, we can only claim to *know* something (rather than just believing blindly) when we can explain *how* we have come to know it, and what justifies our claims that it is true.

13 Graham Harman, as quoted in conversation with Martin Clark and Steven Claydon, at Platform Presents *The Noing Uv It,* at Bergen Kunsthall, 10 January 2015.

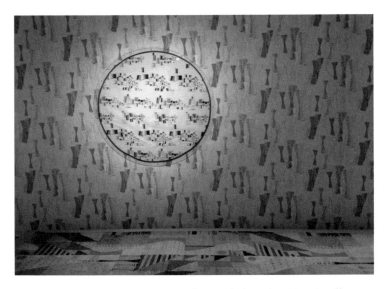

Installation view; *Decorum - Carpets and tapestries by artists*. Marc Camille Chaimowicz wallpaper; Carol Rama, Tovaglia (Nappe) 1951, painted tablecloth and plexiglass; Gunta Stölzl, Geknüpfter Bodenläufer, 1923, wool and hemp carpet. Foto: Marianne Zamecznik

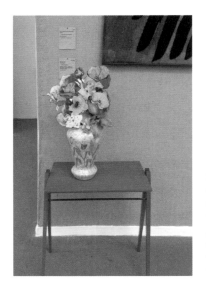

Installation view; *Decorum - Carpets and tapestries by artists*. Marc Camille Chaimowicz, *Tulip vase with bouquet* (2013) glass and paper. Maxim Old side table, ca 1954. Cherrywood table (made by joinery workshop Guy, Boubon-Lancy) Photo: Marianne Zamecznik

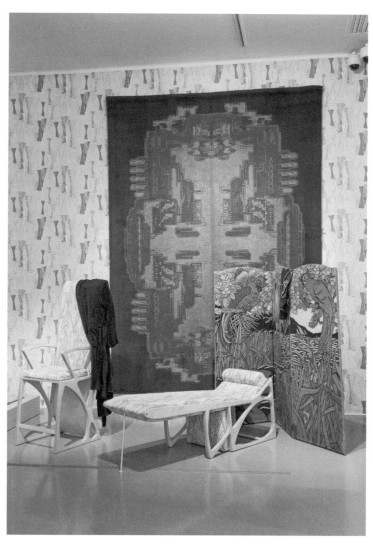

Installation view; *Decorum - Carpets and tapestries by artists*. Marc Camille Chaimowicz (furniture and wall paper), Robert Marie Quesnel (screen), Anonymous (Dutch carpet). Photo: Raphaël Chipault & Benjamin Soligny

It relates to us and to other things in the world. It's not 'alive' but it has agency, it creates innumerable connections around it. Depending on how we choose to present an object in an exhibition, we can allude to its different possibilities and connections to other things; we can love it.

Decorum

An exhibition that in my opinion succeeded in alluding to the possibilities of the object – one which, in the widest sense, loved them by creating a multitude of connections with other things in the world – was the group exhibition *Decorum: Carpets and Tapestries by Artists*[14]. Operating thematically rather than chronologically, textile works by modern and contemporary artists rubbed shoulders with anonymous pieces in ways that confused the eye and made it challenging to separate the works from each other. Through its radical display, the exhibition evoked the original or implied domestic uses of textiles, and in so doing, presented tapestry as the perfect third way between the 'major' and 'minor' arts. It appeared as an art form oscillating between traditional and radical expressions. In her catalogue essay, curator Anne Dressen sheds light on the exhibition strategy:

> It seemed obvious that the exhibition should be considered a collective, transversal effort, like the collaboration between the painter, the weaver, the dyer, and the person commissioning the work. And so, working with architect Christine Ilex Beinemeier, Marc-Camille Chaimowicz, an artist who has always asserted the decorative aspect of his conceptual approach, has decided to enhance the scenography of the exhibition with props that act as triggers for fictional narratives and remind us of the (original or implied) domestic uses of the works. The programme of 'furniture music' put together by Jean-Philippe Antoine is similarly intended to fill out the exhibition and to bring out foreground and background, the relief and the recesses of the rugs and tapestries. Addressing the history of art obliquely enables approaches to rethinking the past, but also a better way of understanding the contemporary. Let's stand up, more than ever, for a speculative materiality.[15]

14 *Decorum: Carpets and Tapestries by Artists* at Musee D'art Moderne de la Ville de Paris (11 October 2013 – 9 February 2014).

15 Anne Dressen: The Transgressive Art of Carpets and Tapestry, or the Return of the Minor, in *Decorum: Carpets and Tapestries by Artists*, Shanghai: Power Station of Art, 2013. (This English catalogue was originally published in French under the direction of Anne Dressen, as *Decorum, Tapis et tapisseries d'artistes* © Éditions Skira Flammarion Paris, 2013.)

In my opinion, the exhibition delivered what it promised; it was able to challenge expectations as to what tapestry could be in a museum. The display was crowded, the labelling was crude, and works were placed 'on top of each other', so as to create dense and synthetic images that inevitably made spotting 'who's who' a greater challenge than if the works had been separated. At the same time, this strategy made the works infinitely more interesting to look at and think about. The interventions by Chaimowicz, consisting of colourful homely objects and wallpapers, made everything gel nicely, as did the exhibition music by Antoine. Perhaps some viewers found these elements disruptive, but for me, they contributed to making *Decorum* a memorable and significant exhibition, precisely because they generated a relevant context and discursive framework where old and new works of art and anonymous objects (often older and non-Western) could continue to grow and produce, constructively critiquing and regenerating themselves, their relation to current discourses, other artworks, the art institution, culture and society.

The new needs friends

If an exhibition can be considered an object in itself, then the annual exhibition *Craft 2014* at KODE – Art Museums of Bergen was an object that got heavily criticized by its critics, mostly due to the exhibition design, conceived by design duo Morten & Jonas. The design consisted of sprayed graffiti and tagging throughout the entire exhibition space, as if a crew had gotten free reign in the galleries, and the works were placed directly against the visually messy surfaces. The sprayed paint was skilfully administered, in a visual language that directly confronted the chasm between 'high' and 'low' art. This obviously gave the displayed craft objects unexpected resistance. I quote Stephen Wright:

> The autonomous sphere was seen as a place where art was free from the overcodes of the general economy and the utilitarian rationality of market society – and as such, something to be cherished and protected. This realm of autonomy was never supposed to be a comfort zone, but the place where art could develop audacious, scandalous, seditious works and ideas – which it set about doing. However, autonomous art came at a cost – one that for many has become too much to bear. The price to pay for autonomy are the invisible parentheses that bracket art off from being taken seriously as a proposition having consequences beyond the aesthetic realm. Art judged by art's

standards can be easily written off as, well... just art. Of contemplative value to people who like that sort of thing, but without teeth. Of course autonomous art has regularly claimed to bite the hand that feeds it; but never very hard.[16]

It seems to me that when Morten & Jonas attempted to allude to the world outside the protected and cherished realm of autonomy, the people who like that sort of thing, that is, the 'protected and cherished realm of autonomy', quickly jumped to defend what, for an annual group-exhibition of contemporary craft, cannot be considered as anything other than a comfort zone.

The design concept was approved and defended by the exhibition jury who held the overall artistic responsibility, but not by some of the artists whose works were featured. Critics wrote harsh reviews, deeming it a completely failed attempt to place crafts in a relevant discursive framework. The message such criticism sends out is that it is risky to challenge conventions and that failure is immanent if one should have the hubris to bring forth bold ideas. I don't think this is the goal of the critics who harshly judge unusual statements, but the result is nevertheless the same. The heated debate made me think of a scene in the Pixar animation *Ratatouille*, where the food critic Anton Ego makes the following deliberation:

> In many ways, the work of a critic is easy. We risk very little yet enjoy a position over those who offer up their work and their selves to our judgment. We thrive on negative criticism, which is fun to write and to read. But the bitter truth we critics must face, is that in the grand scheme of things, the average piece of junk is probably more meaningful than our criticism designating it so. But there are times when a critic truly risks something, and that is in the discovery and defence of the new. The world is often unkind to new talent, new creations. The new needs friends.[17]

It's important to make exhibitions like *Craft 2014*, even if it's scary.

The systemic error
Why is it that so many exhibitions are predictable and thought out? For Martin Clark, the new director of Bergen Kunsthall, the most boring way to make a work of art or an exhibition is when you already have a prescribed idea about what you are going to do and you just set

---

16 Stephen Wright: Toward A Lexicon for Usership.
17 Ratatouille, Pixar Animation Studios, Walt Disney Pictures (2007).

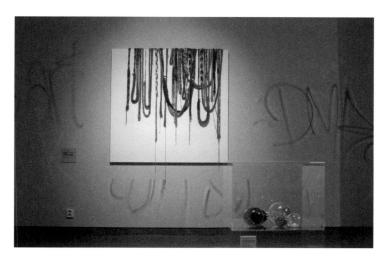

Installation view, *Crafts 2014* at KODE – Art Museums in Bergen. On the wall: Synnøve Øyen: *I hagen, på stranda, hos naboen, ved brønnen*, 2014. In front: Ine Kristine Hove: *Vegg i vegg – plutselig sammenheng*, 2014. Exhibition design: Morten & Jonas. Photo: André Gali

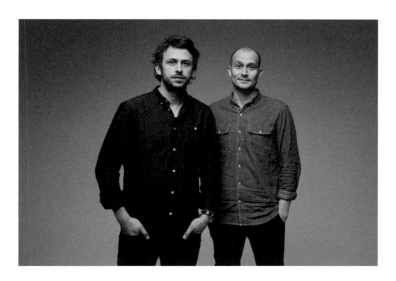

Morten & Jonas is a design duo in Bergen and responsible for the exhibition design for *Crafts 2014* at KODE – Art Museums in Bergen. Photo: Montag

out to produce it. It's boring, says Clark, mostly because it's a reductive, illustrative way of working. As he sees it, 'it's a systemic pressure from the art system, whereby the only way you are going to be able to make an exhibition is if you, two years ahead, tell the institution very clearly what it is about and who is going to be in it'.[18] Clark curated the group show *The Noing Uv It* together with artist Steven Claydon. Its starting point was their discussion about OOO [19] and *Riddley Walker*, a novel written in the late 1970s by Russell Hoban. This story is set some 2,000 years after a nuclear apocalypse, amongst a primitive society that has slowly emerged from the devastation. The book is written in a broken-down, phonetic vernacular, based on the recollection of a worn-down English. The new society is structured around an elaborate 'destruction' myth, which combines mis-remembered history with myths. The exhibition brings together large number of artists' works, as well as objects such as trilobites,[20] the most successful beings in natural history, in terms of their ability to adapt to shifting conditions. While the exhibition is not about the book, it uses the book poetically to develop ideas that concern the nature of matter as well as 'the withdrawn and flickering operation of objects', the evolution of consciousness and 'a climate of orbiting signifiers aggravating around objects'.[21] The idea that an object has a flickering nature appeals to me. The exhibition looks less like a museum show than usual; the works are installed in close proximity to each other, creating blurred distinctions between what is what – one critic calculated that the main gallery space contained forty pieces by eighteen artists. The works in the show are selected and displayed according to a principle of similarity; one piece resembles the other or alludes to the other, rather than being a completely random set up (which seems to be the case with most group shows). Now for me this is interesting – to connect works on the basis of how they look and what they do, and less on the basis of what they

18   Martin Clark, as quoted in conversation with Graham Harman and Steven Claydon at Platform Presents *The Noing Uv It,* at Bergen Kunsthall, 10 January 2015.
19   Object-oriented ontology, as discussed above.
20   Fossil group of extinct marine arthropods.
21   Steven Claydon, quoted in conversation with Graham Harman and Martin Clark, at Platform Presents *The Noing Uv It*, at Bergen Kunsthall, 10 January 2015.

'are about'. On the one hand, it's almost like a child's game of grouping similar forms, but it allows you to approach an artwork very directly, as a physical fact in front of you, and simultaneously, it opens up a space between the artistic intention and the work's own physical force.

As the result of a three-year conversation between the two curators, the exhibition is divided into three chapters that will unfold in 2015. At a panel discussion in connection with the exhibition opening, the two curators discussed the way in which OOO offers a new understanding of what contemporary art is or can be. When asked about whether the exhibition emanated from a specific curatorial process, Clark stated that 'making an exhibition like this is much more about feeling your way and allowing the exhibition as an object to live', emphasizing that working in this way is a privilege. He concluded that 'we have to think about how we can produce these spaces where you can work like this'.

Hear, hear. I believe that contemporary craft has a lot to gain by producing spaces where exhibitions and different forms of dissemination can be treated as dynamic, flickering objects in themselves – where one can take risks as to how objects and ideas are presented and distributed. In doing so, the field of contemporary craft will enhance its ability to produce new discourses as well as new, more inventive and sensitive forms of cultural activity and to carry it out in real-life contexts.

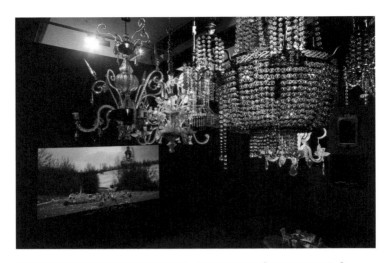

Installation view, *Size Matters* at Kode – Art Museums of Bergen, 2011. Left: Morgan Schagerberg's video work *The City and the Countryside* (2009), in front/ceiling: chandeliers from the museum's collection.

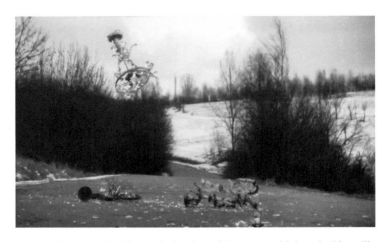

Morgan Schagerberg's video work *The City and the Countryside* (2009), video still.

Crafting Museum Exhibitions: Use or Abuse of Artworks

Anne Britt Ylvisåker

In autumn 2011, the museum I work for, KODE – Art Museums of Bergen, presented Morgan Schagerberg's video work *The City and the Countryside* (2009) in the self-produced exhibition *Size Matters*. The video was projected over almost the entire breadth of one gallery wall, and showed a tranquil, undulating and somewhat monotonous landscape, periodically interrupted by a prism-chandelier being dropped in front of the camera lens and smashing on the ground. In addition, glass prisms were scattered on the gallery floor in front of the video projection. These prisms were part of the work. The seven huge chandeliers hanging in the middle of the room, however, were not. Neither was the group of miniature furniture that was placed under them, nor the mirrors on all the other walls of the room: these objects were carefully selected from KODE's own collections and placed in the exhibition by the museum's curatorial group.

The public did not necessarily differentiate between the video work and the museum's own objects. To the contrary; many viewers saw the video, the chandeliers, the strewn prisms and the miniature furniture as one coherent installation – and they loved it! Favourable comments flowed from many visitors, and KODE's staff could proudly lean back and be pleased at having once again produced a successful exhibition. So far so good.

Afterwards, however, I have reflected over what we actually did.[1] Who, for example, was the *main* artist behind what the public encountered and experienced in the gallery room – the artist of the video work,

---

[1] The article develops thoughts presented at the conference *Sensuous Knowledge*, 25 January 2013, at Bergen Academy of Art and Design. http://www.khib.no/norsk/kunstnerisk-utviklingsarbeid/the-sensuous-knowledge-conference/sk-7-presentations-in-group-sessions/ anne-britt-ylvisaaker/

or the museum's curatorial group? How should the museum deal with the at-times blurred boundary between art production and curatorial approaches? Where is the boundary between 'use' and 'abuse' when putting an artwork into such contexts?

When I, in the following, look more closely at this constellation of problems, I do so from the perspective of a museum-world insider. After having followed the museal life of craft art from the inside for almost 20 years, it is my considered opinion that such art enters into a circulatory pattern within the museum, one which presents different challenges and possibilities than in the wider field of art, and which I believe can be worthwhile reflecting over.

Artwork versus museum object

Let us return to the exhibition room in *Size Matters* and look more carefully at the exhibition's elements. A contemporary work – we know the name of the artist and the year the work was produced – was placed together with pieces of furniture that were removed from a home environment anno 1900 and incorporated into the museum's collections. The furniture represents a time-frame of about 300 years, from the early 1600s to the late 1800s, but none of the pieces have a clear provenance – the museum does not know for sure where they came from originally, when they were made or who produced them. It could seem as though the artwork and the exhibited furniture had nothing in common other than that they were coincidentally in the same room at the same time.

From my perspective it looks different. For me, all the objects and the artwork have a shared characteristic: they all, at one time or another, become museum objects at KODE, thus becoming part of the same museum collection. This means they were removed from the context for which they were originally intended, which had its own set of functions, rules and conventions. As museum objects, they were first decontextualized from that context, then recontextualized into a museum context.

What are the consequences of this? Shagerberg's video work – like all works in the museum collections – receives an additional role as a museum object; by virtue of this role, it faces demands and expectations above and beyond that of simply being a work of art. Should this fact affect what we who are museum curators allow ourselves to do when we want to use and exhibit contemporary works from the museum's collections? In the example from *Size Matters*, all the museum objects were treated in the same way; they could therefore be read as equally important parts of the exhibition. Or is it reasonable to expect that we should behave differently towards the contemporary works the museum owns than we do towards all the other objects we own? If the answer is yes, then this prompts another question: Why? Is it because we want to treat contemporary works differently, because we are expected to do so, or because contemporary works have unique qualities that force us to treat them differently? As a museum curator, I see this as an important, yet strangely enough, absent discussion.

What possibilities, limitations and challenges arise when an artwork changes from only being an independent, contemporary work to *also* being a museum object? Here it may be useful to speak in terms of a two-part research question: the first part concerns what happens in connection with an acquisition – the process whereby a work enters a museum collection – and secondly, what happens when it is removed from storage, exhibited and made available to the public in an exhibition.

Let me elucidate what I mean through some specific, relatively current examples, which give insight into evaluations and decisions that are part of a museum's everyday life. In 2002, the museum for which I work purchased the artwork *Påkledd* (*Dressed*, 2002) by Mari Røisamb, which was being featured an exhibition in the museum. It consisted of eight potatoes dressed in textile outfits. During the exhibition period, the potatoes shrivelled and sprouts began growing through the holes in the clothing. This development was intended by the artists, and for her, it was an important aspect of the work. After the exhibition, the work could not, without further ado, be put in the museum's magazine because the rotting process would affect other works and put the collections at risk. After a thorough discussion with the artist, we agreed that each textile could be carefully split open to remove the potatoes. We also agreed on the procedure for when *Påkledd* would be exhibited in future: on the size, form and colour of the replacement potatoes. Based on this agreement, the conservation department was able to prepare the work for its inclusion in *KODE samtid – JEG* (*KODE Contemporary – I*) in spring 2014.

Some years later, the museum purchased Monica Marcella Kjærstad's *Drømmejobb* (*Dream Job*) and *Drittjobb* (*Shit Job*) (both from 2007). These are tiny, hand-modelled excavating machines in

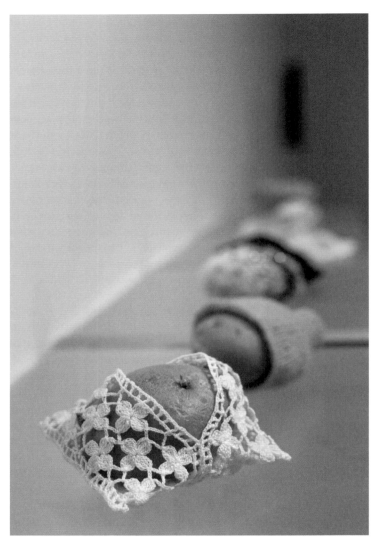

Mari Røisamb: *Påkledd* (*Dressed*, 2002) from the exhibition *KODE samtid – JEG!*
(Kode contemporary – I!) at Kode – Art Museums of Bergen, 2014.

porcelain, balanced respectively on a pile of chocolate and a pile of unfired clay. The museum received only the excavating machines and instructions regarding the chocolate and clay: if the works are exhibited, each pile must consist of a minimum of 250 kilos of new material, roughly assembled. KODE therefore received two incomplete works, which, in an exhibition context, must be completed by the museum. The artist, for her part, must trust that KODE has the capability and will to carry out its part of the agreement without depleting the expression or significantly altering the concept.

I present these examples to point out that not all artworks have a finalized form when they enter a museum collection – neither as far as the artist nor the museum is concerned. Their boundaries become mutable once they become museum objects, and it is up to the museum to finish the works as much as possible each time they are exhibited. That said, *Påkledd, Drømmejobb* and *Drittjobb* are object-based works, and it is not too difficult to know what needs to be done in order to prepare them for an exhibition.

Artist versus curator

The museum will face greater challenges when it mounts the recently-purchased installation *Uten tittel* (*Untitled*, 2014) by Siri Ensrud. In the exhibition in Fredrikstad from which *Uten tittel* was purchased, one saw meter upon meter of electrical wire, carefully entwined with cotton thread, creeping along the mouldings of walls and floors, branching horizontally and vertically across walls, then re-combined through several gallery rooms. The plug and wall-socket were at one end of the electrical cord; at the other end was a lit lightbulb. The installation was fragile, delicate and appealing to the senses. I met Ensrud while she was mounting the work, and she told me she was concerned about how it entered into dialogue with the room, that she thus far had suffered several failed attempts to mount it and was hunting for the optimal expression. It was a matter of trial and error, evaluation and renewed attempts. Now at KODE, there is a box containing 70 meters of thread-entwined cord, along with a written agreement on how the work can be used in future. But how will the museum be able to mount the work as sensitively as the artist, who struggled so hard to mount it in Fredrikstad? In other similar situations, artists often suggest that the best solution is to involve them in mounting the work in future. Theoretically, this is a good idea. But from the museum's perspective, it is short-sighted – therefore unsatisfactory. The various institutions which today comprise KODE have a history dating back approximately 130-140 years, and as a staff member, I am daily confronted with the fact that we operate within a larger time-frame than do most of the people with whom we work. The museum will probably outlive today's artists as well as the staff members who can glean first-hand information from them.

Completely different challenges arise in relation to works that are dependent on a particular type of technical equipment – as is the case with Shagerberg's video *The City and the Countryside*. It arrived at KODE in the form of a computer disc with a file that was unreadable on available equipment. It had to be converted to a different format before it could be projected on the wall in *Size Matters*. Can this be problematic? The result of each and every conversion will be some-what different from that of the previous format. Shagerberg's work, therefore, such as it was shown in *Size Matters* in 2011 at KODE, did not contain exactly the same digital information as the work that was purchased for the museum at the Høstutstillingen (national annual fall exhibition) two years earlier. How many format conversions can a digital work tolerate before it becomes so changed that it becomes a different work? Is it possible, without further ado, to convert a work from an analogue to a digital format and show it on corresponding equipment without there being dramatic consequences for the experience of the work? Who decides where the boundary lies – the artist or the curator? We are talking here about an artwork undergoing change, where the museum's strategies for meeting the challenges that involuntarily attend this type of work can be decisive for how the work, at whatever time, looks in an exhibition.

Let's take an example of a work that never entered KODE's collections: in 2004, *Lounge* (2004), which was created by the Bergen-based artist group TEMP, was offered to the museum. This large installation consisted of hundreds of parts: paper cartons, furniture, photographs, ceramic pieces (also broken ceramics), food scraps and a pictorial series projected on the wall with an old-fashioned slide projector. The museum declined the offer. But not necessarily because *Lounge* was bad or uninteresting to have in our holdings. We rejected it because we could only preserve parts of it for posterity. The installation as a whole would be lost.

As a thought-experiment, what if the museum had incorporated *Lounge* into its collections? What would we have preserved? Everything? A selection of elements? If the latter, what should have been selected and who should have done the selecting? And how should we make this unique artwork accessible to the public in, say, fifty years' time? After all, exhibiting works that were acquired long ago is what the museum normally does. This installation that the museum rejected is now included in the collection of SKMU Sørlandets Kunstmuseum in Kristiansand. Their acquisition committee came to a different conclusion than ours. It chose to see the work as a museum object, but only after doing a thorough evaluation that included a dialogue with TEMP about how the transformation process could or should unfold. According to the then-director of SKMU Sørlandets Kunstmuseum, Erlend Høyersten, the committee decided the installation was within the boundaries of what was possible to exhibit, as long as there was sufficient room for manoeuvre and the possibility of re-creating the work in a way that was fitting for the museum.

TEMP, for its part, had no problem accepting these conditions for a prospective purchase, and, in the mounting instructions that attended the work, expressed 'full confidence that a curator is capable of evaluating new ways of combining the elements and of what will function best in the given context'. In other words, it will be up to the museum and the curator to decide how the work is exhibited in future. The museum becomes an active co-creator of the work, and it is the museum's interpretation of the work that the public sees.

There are two reasons why I focus so thoroughly on the interface between the contemporary artwork and the museum. First, I deem it important to stress that the nature of certain contemporary works is such that they must be recreated to a greater or lesser extent each time they are exhibited. Secondly, this completion of the work, in most cases, is not done by the artist. When the artist delivers the work to the museum, he or she simultaneously relinquishes control over how the final work will look in future exhibitions. Many aspects can of course be regulated through contractual agreements, but this will almost always involve discretion to a greater or lesser extent.

As mentioned introductorily, an extra set of expectations, rules and conventions applies to an artwork that becomes a museum object. I believe it is well recognized that museums are very concerned about preserving the objects such that they remain in as stable a condition as possible. We turn down the lights, don white cotton gloves and cover fragile works with plates of glass. But the fact that we also function as co-creators of certain works is perhaps not fully recognized, either by artists or the wider public.

Nevertheless, this fact of co-creation distinguishes certain contemporary works from traditional museum objects because it forces the museum to treat them differently. It is unnecessary to ask where a chandelier, chair or cup begins and ends. Such objects are already defined and can be placed directly in an exhibition. Perhaps this quality makes it easy to see traditional museum objects as more static and unchangeable than temporal contemporary works that must be created anew each time they are exhibited. This is probably the case if we only take into consideration the physical aspects; the substances themselves. We who work closely with museum objects, however, notice that museal life in itself gives objects a more complex existence. They are used in numerous ways and in diverse contexts. In one sense, a traditional museum object has something ephemeral and fluid about it that can resemble the qualities of certain contemporary works. But not in the same way – quite the contrary: while the substance in a traditional museum object is more or less static and stable, the substance in a contemporary work, as the examples above show, can be ephemeral and/or mutable. On the other hand: there where the role of a traditional museum object is varied and dynamic, the role of many contemporary works will be more static. An ephemeral artwork has a hear-and-now character that largely hinders it from moving in and out of roles and contexts without it simultaneously being created anew.

The artist's agenda versus the museum's agenda

Swedish ceramist Kjell Rylander is fascinated by the transformation process an artwork undergoes when it becomes a museum object. He draws this process in as a possible reading of the work *Portrait of the Anonymous* (2010), which was part of his research project *Archives* (2012) at Kunsthøgskolen i Bergen (Bergen Academy of Art and Design). When KODE acquired this work, the decision was motivated by the way *Portrait of the Anonymous* sheds light on – or perhaps it is more accurate to say 'how it blurs' – the boundaries between the artworld and the museum world, between the work and the prop, and between the work's existence in the exhibition and in storage. When first encountering this work in an art gallery, we saw, on a lacquered-steel storage

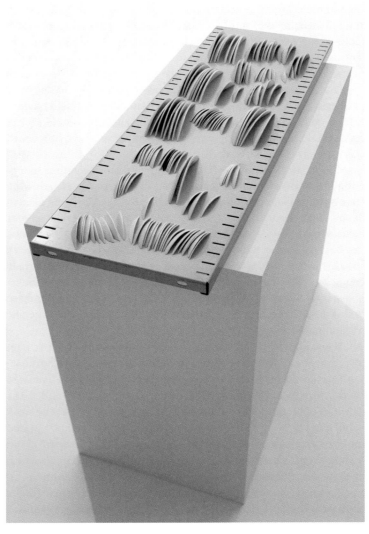

Kjell Rylander: *Portrett av det anonyme* (Portrait of the anonumous), 2010.
Porselen, metall, tre. Tilhøyrer Kunstmuseene i Bergen. Photo: Øystein Klakegg

shelf, more than 100 porcelain plate fragments organized in groups and balanced on one edge. Our amazement was immense when we received the work – including the underlying plinth. Had the art gallery made a mistake? No – when we called Rylander to explain the mistake, he informed us that the plinth was part of the work. Not only that: the fact that museum personnel called him because they were uncertain about what belonged to the work and what was just a random exhibition prop strengthened his conviction that this simple, white-painted and slightly dirty plinth made with inexpensive fibreboard was truly part of his artwork.

Despite confusion over the plinth, the artist's intentions in creating the work and the museum's intentions in purchasing it were largely the same in this particular instance. But such does not need to be the case. The artist and museum can just as easily have divergent ideas about what defines a work, what its relevant interpretations can be, and they can have different expectations for how the work should function in the museal context. It is presupposed that artists create works based on their own inner motivation and ideas, but it is easier to overlook the fact that each and every museum purchase is also made in order to fit with or develop the profile of the specific museum collection.

When an artwork crosses the museum's threshold, it does so not merely in order to fulfil the artist's intentions, but to support the museum's ambitions for what it wants to be and how it will fulfil its role in society. When KODE, for example, acquired Schagerberg's video *The City and the Countryside*, it did so based on the idea that the work could shed light on the older collections of decorative and applied art. When presented to the public in the right way, the work could incite reflection on the history of the museum's collections, but also on how society in general administers and stewards its common cultural heritage. According to the museum, the work can be read from a meta-perspective that treats the role of the museum as a core element. This reading is not necessarily self-evident – it could be irrelevant or above and beyond any reading the artist considers relevant. If so, are the artist's intentions for the work superior to the museum's intentions for making the acquisition – or the opposite?

Roles and expectations

In the article 'Translating Knowledge, Translating Cultures', the historian Peter Burke rejects the idea that cultural heritage can be transferred directly from one cultural field to another and still be meaningful:

> [It] has become increasingly apparent in the last generation, in studies ranging from sociology to literature, that 'reception' is not passive but active. Ideas, information, artefacts and practices are not simply adopted but on the contrary, they are adapted to their new cultural environment. They are first decontextualized and then recontextualized, domesticated or 'localized'. In a word, they are 'translated'. ... Translators learn to live with a dilemma: should they be faithful to the original text from which they are translating, or intelligible to the readers of the text they are writing? [2]

Following from the domestication scenario, the translator has relatively free reign and is a co-creator of the end-product.

Burke's theory is also relevant in KODE's context and in relation to the theme under discussion. According to my understanding, he turns me into a translator, by virtue of my position as a museum curator who participates in acquiring contemporary artworks from the artworld and incorporating them into the museum context. In moving cultural expressions from one cultural arena to another, I am familiar with the dilemma Burke outlines: In my everyday practice, should I primarily be concerned about the artwork as an autonomous entity, or should I instead concentrate on strategies that will enable the artwork's role as a museum object to come to the fore? In other words, how is it possible to balance the artwork's own presence and expression with the exhibition architect's professional creativity and the story the museum curator wants to tell? The finalized exhibition, after all, is the result of contributions from many professional groups, each with their own ambitions for their professional work.

Theoretically, there is a clear distinction between the artist, the exhibition architect and the museum curator: the artist is responsible for producing the artwork (at the very least, for organizing its

---

2   Peter Burke: Translating Knowledge, Translating Cultures. In Michael North (ed.), *Kultureller Austausch: Bilanz und Perspektiven der Frühneuzeitforschung*, Köln, Weimar, Wien: Böhlau Verlag GMBH & CIE, 2009, pp. 69-77.

production); the curator is responsible for procuring the artwork for the museum's collections, and to exhibit it periodically – often through collaboration with an exhibition architect. My specific examples and Burke's ideas about translating cultural expressions show that the distinction between these roles is far less obvious. Quite the reverse; it is easy to find similarities between an artist's creativity and various aspects of curatorial practice. The main difference is perhaps the attitude towards the artwork: the artwork represents the culmination of the artist's efforts, but for the museum curator and exhibition architect, it functions as a kind of 'raw material' and means for achieving another end, an exhibition. This brings us back to *Size Matters* and the question I asked introductorily: did KODE misuse Schagerberg's artwork in that exhibition?

During the exhibition period, three art critics commented on the show and how it reflected various answers to the given question. Tommy Olsson was the most positive critic, at the same time as he was aware that the whole of the exhibition was hierarchically superior to the experience of any individual artwork:

> The apparently random combination of works from different epochs, paradoxically enough, helps underscore the extent to which this is a curated exhibition. The show is so strictly and deliberately curated that this drastic displacement of what an exhibition in fact is, manages to create a singular electric tension: sometimes the actual placement of an object generates more meaning than the object's presence as a work of art.[3]

While Olsson allowed himself to be amazed and seduced by the exhibition concept, the two other critics were more reserved about the results, yet for quite divergent reasons: Sigrun Åsebø argued that the museum's love of contextualization, compositions and forms of presentation – precisely what Olsson considered positive – was far too steering and disruptive. In the given framework, the public had neither the tranquillity nor the space for personal reflection on individual

---

3   Tommy Olsson: Størrelsen på utstillingen. In *Kunstkritikk,* 18 October 2011. (Accessed 19 December 2014) http://kunstkritikk.no/kritikk/ storrelsen-pa-utstillingen/.

works.[4] Anne Marthe Dyvi, however, was not negative towards the fact that the exhibition concept dominated the works, but asserted that the message the museum wanted to put across through its exhibition concept was far too vague:

> What is the museum trying to do? Measure the sizes of things: in relation to what? Are these just some things seen in relation to other things, or are they things that put something at risk? The museum doesn't want to dictate what the public should experience, but I want to know more about what arises at the interface between the things, and which has caused the curators to present exactly these tableaux. Someone has chosen and composed these tableaux, chosen the lighting and given the exhibition a framework: Why?[5]

One critic thought we had a good exhibition strategy; another thought that same strategy did not result in meaning. In our present context, however, perhaps the most interesting feature of the criticism was to note that one critic, Åsebø, primarily focused on the artworks and how difficult it was for the public to experience them in the given context. As such, her sentiments parallel those of the Danish museologist Camilla Mordhorst, who argues that museums' eagerness to use museum objects in order to represent something above and beyond the objects themselves results in overlooking how important the direct encounter with the works themselves is.[6] To encounter a museum object 'face-to-face' affects our senses and does something with us and the way we experience the world.

Both Olsson and Dyvi, as I understand them, saw the exhibition rooms in *Size Matters* more as places for interaction – a battle field, as it were – between presenting artworks qua artworks and presenting them as the museum objects which they also are. As museum objects, they enter into contexts that render them more than simply themselves. This is a key point as far as I am concerned, for I believe it is precisely

---

4 Sigrun Åsebø: Stort og godt. Exhibition review of 'Ting, Tang, Trash' at Permanenten, Vestlandske kunstindustrimuseum and 'Size Matters' at Bergen Art Museum, *Bergens Tidende*, 4 October, 2011.

5 Anne Marthe Dyvi: Mus eller elefant? In *Kunstforum* 03 October 2011. (Accessed 19 December 2014). http://kunstforum.as/2011/10/mus-eller-elefant/.

6 Camilla Mordhorst: The Power of Presence: The 'Cradle to Grave' Installation at the British Museum. *Museum and Society* 7, no. 3 (2009), pp. 194-205.

here, in the field of friction between contemporary art and the museum world, that the art museum has a unique position and possibility to fulfil its most important role in society.

The philosopher Boris Groys, in his article 'On the New', also believes the art museum plays a central role in the development of contemporary art.[7] Older art, he claims, does not need a museum. By virtue of its age, the necessary distance to reality has already been established in order for it to be perceived as art. The situation is completely different for contemporary art, the primary characteristic of which is that it does not significantly distinguish itself from everyday life. Both *Lounge* and *The City and the Countryside* can function as good examples of what Groys is talking about. In these cases, the museum has a much more important function – yes, it is absolutely essential, he argues. To begin with, the art museum can create distance between contemporary artworks and everyday life in a way that enables viewers to see the artworks for what they are: contemporary artworks. But according to Groys, the museum is also absolutely crucial for contemporary art's further development. This is because the museum, through its work, renders completely normal things unique, furnishing objects with an additional value that they do not enjoy in everyday life. Groys calls this 'a difference beyond difference'.

History writing, Groys asserts, is a dynamic process that involves editing the boundaries between life and death; between the new, part of which is contemporary art, and the old, which has already ended up in the museum. In this competition to create history, the museum functions as an editor or border guard, and the artists both create their works and are evaluated in relation to the same boundaries.

I am both fascinated and flattered by the central position Groys awards those of us who work in art museums and our role in developing contemporary art. I can also follow his argumentation to a certain extent, but I do not completely recognize the picture he creates, and I believe he has lost sight of an important point: the art museum, as an arena for discussing and negotiating history, does not fulfil its mission when works are added to the museum collections, nor do I think works are 'dead' after they enter the collections. Quite the contrary.

---

7   Boris Groys: On the New. *Artnodes* (December 2002): upaginated. (Accessed 19 December 2014) http://www.uoc.edu/artnodes/espai/eng/art/groys1002/ groys1002.html.

From my perspective, to cross the threshold of an art museum in order to become a museum object is just the beginning of an artwork's completely new, nomadic life. For the rest of its museal existence, it will be used in many ways. It will play different roles and move in and out of different contexts.

I believe it is one of the art museum's foremost duties to do research on the artwork in itself, on art history, and on the museum's position and history, and to do so over and over again. This exercise, however, does not necessarily mean we do research on all the diverse aspects simultaneously. The alternation between the different gazes creates the dynamic in our work. From the museum's perspective, it is therefore most correct to say that artworks, first and foremost, function as potential material for us, and must acquiesce to being used in highly divergent ways adapted to a wide range of research topics. In some contexts, the works will absolutely be able to play the main role. In other contexts their role will be to illustrate something far different than what they are in themselves.

An artwork is subjected to ever new readings, and based upon this perspective, I have a problem with Boris Groys' claim that it is 'dead' as soon as it enters a museum's collection and becomes part of history. I argue that the work merely enters a different phase in its life. The artworld is not alone in being challenged by, and having to formulate an opinion on, redefinitions of its boundaries in the development of 'the new'. The art museum is also forced to do soul searching and to engage in innovative thinking if it wants to be a relevant actor in society.

The Norwegian archaeologist Bjørnar Olsen points out how things gain value and meaning through the way in which they are made, used and exchanged.[8] Meanwhile, the same production, use and exchange will also leave traces of meaning and value for all who are involved in the process. What is more: the relation between a thing and its creator, the public, the curator and/or the collector will naturally be relevant more than once in the thing's existence. It will gain meaning through all the different social interactions it participates in, and there will be negotiations about different significations as long as the thing exists – also when it is no longer extant. In this way, the biography of human

---

8   Bjørnar Olsen: Material Culture after Text: Re-membering Things. *Norwegian Archaeological Review 36*, no. 2 (2003), pp. 87-104.

beings and the biography of the things we surround ourselves with will intermingle and mutually influence each other's formation.

I see this approach as an interesting alternative to Groys' ideas. If we transfer Olsen's theory about the relation between things and human beings to artworks and museums, it would mean that each and every interaction between a museum and a specific artwork will add yet another layer of history and insight to both the artwork and the museum. The museum and the artwork will help to mutually develop each other, and the interaction between being perceived as an artwork and as a museum object will, from my perspective, add a new dimension to the continuous process surrounding the work's 'biography'.

And to answer the question I asked in the introduction: yes, an acquisition of a 'difficult' contemporary artwork can require that the museum personnel must make some decisions which, in some points, differ from the decisions we normally make, based on the character of the specific work. But this primarily concerns the work's physical aspects. Regarding the way the museum uses artworks; I do not see that we must act differently towards contemporary artworks than we do towards all the other objects in the collections.

Misuse? No. An art museum is not an art gallery, and according to my lights, it should not try to act like one. The unique position the art museum is in, on account of its collections, enables it to draw forth works from the magazine and to challenge them, but also the museum and the public, over and over again. This is what we should do. Merely by handling artworks as museum objects, in addition to whatever else they are, the art museum will fulfil its role in society.

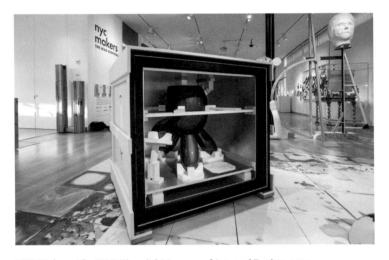

NYC Makers: The MAD Biennial. Museum of Arts and Design, 2014.
Photo: Eric Scott.Captions

From Me to You:
A Personal Account of
Craft Curation

Glenn Adamson

There are some things in life – dogs, country music, Marmite, Jeff Koons – that people either love, or to which they express hatred, antipathy or indifference. Polarizing things can inspire strong convictions about taste and lifestyle. Craft is one of these things. People either absolutely love it, or they are completely indifferent.

I have met many partisans of the handmade, and many opponents. The partisans often complain of being marginalized and disregarded, particularly in comparison to other fields such as fine art and design. The opponents are perhaps less animated by conscious enmity and more by casual (perhaps thoughtless) disrespect. This goes a long way back, to the days of the Industrial Revolution, when writers who advocated for the factory system routinely maligned handwork as inefficient and backward. These writers had an unfortunate tendency to put words like 'mere' in front of craft, implying that it was not truly important – it was just a pathway, not a destination.

One consequence of this dynamic is that craft today tends to be curated in a spirit of advocacy. The exhibitions try to establish the validity of the handmade as such, and often they do so stridently. The curator's strategy may be to support specific makers or to make a more general case for craft in ethical, aesthetic or political terms. A few examples – all shows I admire greatly – include *Gestures of Resistance* at the Museum of Contemporary Craft in Portland, Oregon (2010, curated by Shannon Stratton and Judith Leemann), *Power of Making* at the V&A in London (2011, curated by Daniel Charny), and *Queer Threads* at the Leslie-Lohmann Museum in New York (2014, curated by John Chaich). These exhibitions, each in their own way, presented craft as a powerful force of aesthetic discovery and social change.

Though I didn't set out to do so, my own record of curating exhibitions follows a very different trajectory – one that does not disregard craft, certainly, but is nonetheless more ambivalent, maybe even cagey about it. Perhaps this reflects my personal relationship to craft, which has developed through writing history and theory more than through making exhibitions. Books and critical essays accommodate complexity and doubt much more readily than do museum shows. This is partly because discursive texts are much more sustained in their argumentation (a good curator remembers that even the best display is just a bunch of stuff in a room, and that visitors may sample it at any speed and in any order they choose). Partly, too, exhibitions happen in institutions that are themselves positive in outlook, as a result of funding structures and obligations of public service. Few curators want their visitors to exit an exhibition feeling skeptical; they want them to fall in love with the place and to return soon.

Now that I'm the director at the Museum of Arts and Design (MAD) in New York rather than an academic or curator, I've been reflecting on these issues from a new point of view. Our institution is as positively-oriented as any – for example, we routinely speak of acting as a platform for creativity, and of upholding the highest standards of quality. We also have an unusually complex relationship to the concept 'craft'. As some readers will know, we were founded as the Museum of Contemporary Crafts in 1956, then later changed our name to the American Craft Museum, and only jettisoned the C-word from our title in 2003. This positions us as a museum with a deep historical commitment to craft, but a very open, perhaps even undefined relationship to the concept in the present. Given my background as a craft specialist, I've been very concerned to address both the history and the present-day situation for craft. I've come to feel that we should no longer think of ourselves as a 'craft museum' in the narrow sense, representing a movement or a set of key media (wood, clay, metal, fibre, wood); but that we should advocate for craft as a pervasive cultural and creative force.

Toward the end of this essay, I will return briefly to this situation and discuss the exhibition *NYC Makers* – the inaugural edition of a new biennial we've initiated here. But first, I want to retrace the steps that took me to MAD in the first place. This means reviewing three other exhibition projects, each of which staked out a different position with respect to craft. In retrospect, I've come to think of these exhibitions as establishing different styles of curating, different motivations. This wasn't in any way a conscious program, and I make no claims to systematic or comprehensive thinking, either in the exhibitions themselves or this essay. Curators are not artists, and curatorial work is reactive more than it is expressive. My curatorial practice is certainly no exception. Each of the exhibitions I will examine here occurred in a particular institutional setting and was significantly affected by that context. Even so, I believe that when seen together, they amount to a sort of portrait of me as a curator and hopefully may suggest to others a few directions craft exhibitions can take. Others with the same opportunities would have curated the shows differently. I speak only from my own experience.

Curating from the Head: Postmodernism

The first exhibition I'd like to talk about is *Postmodernism: Style and Subversion, 1970 to 1990*, which opened at the V&A in the autumn of 2011. This was the largest of the projects I have curated in my career, and by no means could it be construed as a craft show. Though it did include objects associated with the studio craft movement in America and Great Britain – ceramics, jewellery, furniture, metalwork and the like – it also covered every other creative discipline we could manage: architecture, design, fashion, graphics, music, painting, sculpture and more. In the process of preparing the exhibition, I found myself confronted by the relative weakness of studio craft in this cross-disciplinary context, and ultimately, by craft's relevance to the broader field of artistic endeavour.

To create *Postmodernism,* I worked with a huge team, most importantly my co-curator at the V&A, Jane Pavitt. We assigned ourselves the task of providing a chronological narrative about postmodern art and design – undertaking that task with considerable trepidation, given that postmodernism's only real rule (first laid down by Jean Francois Lyotard) was 'no grand narratives'. Still, all histories have a shape, however fragmentary, and we aimed to give one to our audience. Set in three large galleries, the exhibition charted a movement from initial academic experimentation (largely in the realm of architecture), through a proliferating subcultural phase (exemplified by pop stars like Grace Jones), to a culminating stage of commercialization and corporatization. The last gallery was chock full of shining luxury commodities, teapots and necklaces, many of them designed by star architects; facing them down was the artist Jenny Holzer's baleful

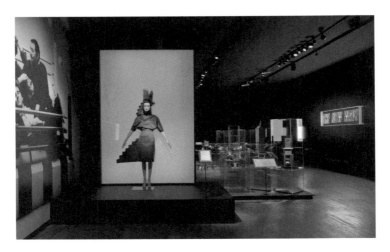

Postmodernism: Style and Subversion, 1970 to 1990. Victoria and Albert Museum, 2011. Exhibition design by Carmody Groarke (architects) and APFEL (graphic designers).

billboard, circa 1985, reading PROTECT ME FROM WHAT I WANT. The takeaway message was that postmodernism had fallen prey to its own logic. Its stylistic and conceptual manoeuvers, once so vividly subversive and antagonistic, had come to seem like just another option in the palette of artists, designers, architects, advertisers and executives. Money, in our show, had the last word.

We might of course have approached the subject differently. Had we not been curating in the shadow of the 2008 economic collapse – Jane and I had our first planning meeting the week that Lehman Brothers announced its bankruptcy – perhaps economics might not have been so prominent in our finale. In a more innocent era we might have been tempted to play it very differently – to create a postmodern exhibition about postmodernism. This might have presented a less straightforward (less 'grand') narrative, one that actually deployed the tactics of irony and self-referentiality that we sought to document. But that seemed both inadvisable and unattractive to us. We were, after all, curating for a mass audience who were not necessarily well-versed in postmodern theory. There seemed little to be gained by making an arch, self-regarding show that eluded its intended visitors.

Anyway, neither Jane (b. 1967) nor I (b. 1972) considered ourselves to be postmodernists, nor even champions of the postmodern position. We were definitely products of the moment. As teenagers we both listened to New Wave music, and even dressed the part (Jane more than me, though I had my moments). As a freshman in college, I was asked to watch and then analyze the quintessential postmodern film *Blade Runner* in no less than three introductory courses. And in graduate school I was fed a steady diet of the aforementioned Lyotard, as well as Jean Baudrillard, Michel Foucault and Jacques Derrida. I was told that postmodernism was over and done with, though what was to replace it was harder to say. That experience doubtless instilled in me a sense of distance from the generation that came before. In the 1970s it was still possible to feel that smashing the ideals of modernism would release enough kinetic energy to fuel a new era. By the 1990s that fuel had been exhausted.

As curators, this put us in the unusual position of working with material that we had no particular desire to celebrate. Though museums have become much more self-conscious places in the past few decades (this in itself is one result of the postmodern turn), it's still unusual for curators to have profoundly mixed feelings about the objects they're displaying. In some ways we loved the content of our show, finding it by turns hilarious, exciting and melancholy. We noted with pleasure the way that postmodern practice anticipated more recent design, for example in the cut-and-paste graphics of the 1970s, which look for all the world as if they were made using the latest version of Photoshop. We were, of course, geekily thrilled to have the famous relics of our own adolescent era on view – David Byrne's 'Big Suit', Grand Master Flash's turntables, original proofs for New Order record sleeves designed by Peter Saville. But there was also something remote about these fragments. A feeling pervaded the galleries, of the party having ended long ago, leaving little behind but a set of difficult questions. Then, too, there were the hollowness and cynicism of much postmodernism, and, as many critics of the V&A show pointed out, the sheer ugliness of most of the forms produced. Postmodernism's paroxysms of self-doubt, its strenuous exaggerations, its healthy kitsch quotient: at the time these qualities were liberating. In retrospect, despite the fascination they exert, it's hard not to be thankful it's all over.

How did craft fit into all this? Not easily. As I've already noted, objects conventionally classed as craft works were only an occasional grace note in the show. We included a few ceramists such as Alison Britton, Carol McNicoll, Peter Shire and Betty Woodman, who took recourse in historicism and decoration as a way out of modernist strictures. There was radically disjunctive handmade furniture by Pieter de Bruyne and Fred Baier (an intended work by Wendell Castle fell by the wayside for reasons of budget), and classic specimens of 1980s excess by the likes of metalworker Richard Mawdsley and ceramist Adrian Saxe. But even these objects, for all their interest, did little to define the narrative of the show.

The more interesting stories about craft lay beneath the surface. We were fascinated to discover that the earliest designs of the Memphis group, which most people take for mass-manufactured objects in cheap materials (plywood and plastic laminate), were actually fabricated by a single skilled cabinetmaker called Renzo Brugola. Postmodern fashion by the likes of Vivienne Westwood and Rei Kawakubo also afforded rich seams of insight about the way traditional pattern-cutting was inverted and distorted for provocative purposes. Graphics by April Greiman and Vaughan Oliver proved to be incredibly intensive and skilled examples of craftsmanship – 'cut and paste' indeed.

The lesson that I took away from the exhibition, then, was that craft per se – framed in terms of a movement or a set of media with partisan support – wasn't all that important to the postmodern episode. In a more tacit, behind-the-scenes fashion, however, craft was absolutely intrinsic to the process of creation. Nothing could have happened in the postmodern hotspots of Milan, Tokyo, New York and London if the experimentalists in those cities hadn't had either skills of their own to rely on, or artisans they could enlist to realize their ideas. Though this isn't an ironclad rule, one could even say that the more handmade a postmodern exemplar was (i.e., when it was still at the stage of a prototype or initial proposal), the more likely it was to carry a critical edge. By the time such insurrectionary ideas found their way to the assembly line – Michael Graves' kettles for Target spring to mind – they were drained of their fighting spirit. In a funny, backwards way, then, *Postmodernism: Style and Subversion, 1970 to 1990* provided ample proof of craft's validity. It's just that this message, like most of the workmanship itself, hovered just beneath the surface.

Curating From the Hip: Fix Fix Fix

At the other end of the logistical spectrum from the *Postmodernism* exhibition was a show I curated the following year called *Fix Fix Fix*, at the invitation of Gallery SO in East London. Its theme was the art of repair, which I pursued through an associative chain of thinking. Executed in a matter of weeks and with very little budget, the show was a single instinctive gesture rather than a sustained research project. It was comprised largely of contemporary objects rather than historical works, and about half of the objects on display were contributed by artists in response to a brief. The challenge I set was to repair an existing object, prioritizing respect for that thing. My original idea was that the participating artists should adhere to a professional standard of repair, which one might call 'anti-expressive' (I was thinking here about the fixed object as a sub-species of the 'assisted readymade', a term introduced by Duchamp to refer to artist-altered found objects). An interesting feature of repair is that it is self-effacing. The perfect fix would restore the broken object to its original state. That is only ever an ideal – even the most skilled restorer cannot turn back time – so fixing is always a matter of approximation. But even so, repair tends to erase itself, all the more so when it's done well.

With these thoughts in mind, alongside the commissioned artworks in *Fix Fix Fix*, I introduced several everyday artefacts that marked out positions in the world of repair. My intention was to create a level playing field where art objects and non-art objects took on equal status. To underline this point, I decided to withhold identification of the works on display from the audience. When viewers encountered a Jeep motor in the middle of the gallery, or a set of nineteenth-century mounts that could be used to repair a piece of French court furniture, or a Japanese porcelain box skilfully mended with lacquer and gold, or the frame of a grand piano hanging in a custom-fabricated steel truss, the public weren't necessarily aware of the status of these things. Were they artworks, or not? I wanted to forestall an answer to that question, in the hope that the question itself would come to seem irrelevant.

Furthermore, I wanted to infuse the exhibition with a complex range of emotional tonalities. These were present in *Postmodernism* too, but I think that the smaller scale and tighter focus of *Fix Fix Fix* yielded a more intense (and possibly contradictory) psychological environment. There was certainly outright celebration in the show – not least in a video made under the aegis of Fixperts. Founded by Daniel Charny (curator of *Power of Making*, mentioned above) and James Corrigan, and now involving a global team of contributors, Fixperts is a social project of sorts. It involves pairing up design professionals with people whose lives can be improved through the fixing of something. This could be as simple as a custom-made wheelchair cushion or as elaborate as a completely redesigned kitchen. The point of the project is to illuminate the rich connections that are brought into being by such maker/client collaborations.

But elsewhere in the show other notes sounded. A bundle of furniture mounts, displayed in a wrapping of paper and string just as I found them in storage at the restoration shop Arlington Conservation, resembled a Dada sculpture. Appropriated (by me, not by an artist) from a non-art context, it was the object in the show that most strongly suggested a Duchampian aesthetic. A Jeep motor, by contrast, evoked the world of the working-class tradesman. It also drew my thoughts to a historical exhibition context, the Museum of Modern Art's 1934 show *Machine Art*, which helped introduce a taste for industrial forms that persists to this day.

A porcelain box repaired with gold and lacquer indexed yet another well-established aesthetic – the reverence shown to precious ceramics in traditional Japanese culture. In that context, an object that has been broken and repaired may actually become more valuable,

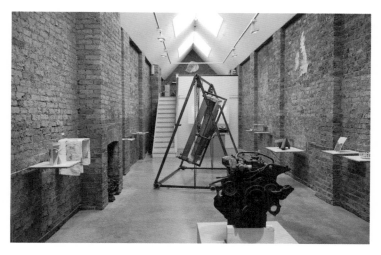

Fix Fix Fix. Gallery SO, London, 2013. Photo: Sipke Visser

because a moment in its lifecycle has been enshrined. Hence the gold repair known in Japan as *kintsugi*: an accident permanently fixed in a resplendent material. Then there was the piano frame. I extracted it from a project undertaken by amateur craftsman Steven Probert. He had inherited the instrument; a grand piano made at the turn of the century by the well-regarded Boston firm Mason and Hamlin, and over the course of many years has dismantled it and remade it to his own exacting specifications. The lengths to which he had gone to achieve the perfect sound are remarkable – not least, in building a steel A-frame to give himself access to all its surfaces, which he has reworked fastidiously, in-filling each nick, scrape or dent with a custom-fashioned wooden inlay.

Walking around *Fix Fix Fix*, I realized that I preferred these various 'non-art' objects far more than the works I had commissioned: they seemed to me more strange, more aesthetically intense, more provocative. This is not to say that artists cannot achieve all these qualities; just that the world already offers them, if we know where to look. As modest as *Fix Fix Fix* was in comparison to any V&A show, including *Postmodernism*, I feel it was just as effective in outlining a curatorial methodology that enabled every object to be treated as equal. This methodology has become more and more common in recent years, though decorative art curators have certainly not been leading the way. Specialists in African and Native American art were among the first to embrace the idea that artefacts, more than just being collected and explained, should be given a second life through the mediating act of display.

The anthropologist Alfred Gell, for example, was deeply impressed by the exhibition *Art/Artifact*, which was curated by Susan Vogel for the Museum for African Art in New York in 1988. He particularly appreciated Vogel's decision to display a hunting net (made by the Zande people of Central Africa) tightly baled and set in the middle of a white cube gallery, looking for all the world as if it were a piece of contemporary art. Gell's response to this gesture was an article entitled 'Vogel's Net: Traps as Artworks and Artworks as Traps',[1] which argued for an 'ecumenical' approach in which objects wouldn't be shown according

---

1   Alfred Gell: Vogel's Net, Traps as Artworks and Artworks as Traps, *Journal of Material Culture* March 1996 vol. 1 no. 1, 15-38.

to a pre-existing category (fine art, craft, ethnographic material), but rather according to their potential to ensnare the audience in a web of interpretative implications. All objects that are 'vehicles of complicated ideas', he wrote, including things like hunting nets that are ostensibly 'pragmatic and technical' in nature, could be equally regarded as suitable objects for aesthetic and conceptual interpretation: 'I would define as a candidate artwork any object or performance that potentially rewards such scrutiny because it embodies intentionalities that are complex, demanding of attention and perhaps difficult to reconstruct fully.'[2]

If *Postmodernism* positioned craft as a backstage operation, *Fix Fix Fix* was nominally more explicit in its advocacy for craft. It was, after all, staged in a venue associated with the field (Gallery SO is primarily known for its presentation of conceptual jewellery and metalwork), and it took one type of making, or re-making, as its subject. In the end, though, the show called the artistic pretentions of craft into question. That motor, that piano frame, seemed to offer a kind of truth that I couldn't easily find in any other way. The experience of doing *Fix Fix Fix* left me wanting that kind of honesty in all my curatorial work. The next project I took on gave me the chance to put it front and centre.

Curating from the Heart: Tenderness

In 2013 I was invited to curate the 40th instalment of a Nordic craft survey called *Tendenser* ('Tendencies'), which was held at the F15 Gallery in Moss, near Oslo. This was the first time that a non-Nordic person was asked to curate the show. It put me in a position where I had to think not only about craft, but about the Nordic region and its creative energies. My original inspiration for the show took two forms, one very superficial – a simple wordplay between the Norwegian word *Tendenser* and the English word *Tenderness* – and the other very profound, at least to me. I had encountered a painting by the Swedish artist Gunnel Wåhlstrand at the Parasol Unit Gallery in London in 2011. The image, rendered in a feather-light ink wash, shows two children sitting in front of a bright, sunny window. It turns out to have been based on a family snapshot – the little boy in the picture is the artist's father, who later committed suicide. It's an extremely moving work of

---

2   Ibid.

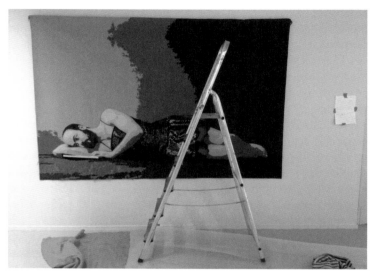

Installing the work of Karina Presttun in *Tenderness*, F15 Galleri, Moss, Norway, 2013. Photo: Glenn Adamson

art, especially when you know the story behind it: the sense of fragile innocence, a past that one can never recapture, is so palpable in it. I happened to be alone when I saw the painting, and it literally brought tears to my eyes. In the same moment, for some reason, I thought of the song *Sentimental Journey*, and I remember standing there with my eyes wet, whistling that song quietly to myself.

That's how the curatorial process started – with a simple, unstudied and emotional reaction. Obviously this was quite different from the approach I took in *Fix Fix Fix*, which was intentionally sly and provocative, or the approach for *Postmodernism*, in which Jane and I assumed the traditional voice of the authoritative and objective curator. With *Tenderness*, I wanted to curate something from the heart, and hopefully convey that to the audience – to create a show that would be felt rather than read.

Galleri F15 is located in a grand country house, so when visitors entered the exhibition, they first encountered a beautiful spiral staircase, original to the property. In this space, they heard the song *Sentimental Journey*, expertly whistled not by me but by one of the gallery staff. It was just a recording, but it sounded like there was someone in the space – or perhaps a ghost from the past. In theory, visitors were also supposed to smell a faint perfume, which I asked the gallery staff to spray intermittently in the space. (In practice, it was so faint as to be positively subliminal, not to say undetectable – these special effects aren't always easy to execute.)

Leaving the stair and hall area, visitors entered a gallery built around the Wåhlstrand painting, which faced them as they entered. I found out as we were installing the exhibition that the building had been occupied by the Nazi military during the Second World War, and that there was a photograph of this room from that time, with several officers standing in it. There is also a white stove in the corner of the space, very classical, very imposing, which was installed by the Germans when they were there. (The Nazis lean against it in the photo, with exactly the kind of arrogant, proprietary attitude you might expect of them.) This unforeseen fact gave additional emotional weight to Wåhlstrand's image, which after all depicts two young blond children from exactly that moment in history. Curators get lucky sometimes.

Around this same room, I asked the artist Mia Göransson to install a series of blush-pink ceramic forms, which look somewhat like alien flowers. I wanted her to decorate the room, and also to metaphorically give these objects to the exhibition and the other artists in the show. I had the thought that this act of generosity might echo the tradition prevalent at art school degree shows – particularly common in the Nordic region – in which friends and family members leave flowers in the corners of the galleries, near students' work. I've often been struck by how this aesthetic and seemingly purposeless material is introduced into a show. It's a gesture of honesty and appreciation that the artworks themselves don't always manifest.

This idea in the show connected to a broader theme of gift-giving. Something that strikes me as extremely important about craft, but which is rarely acknowledged in the institutional infrastructure devoted to it, is its role in family circles. A handmade present – even one that is store-bought, but much more so one made by the giver – provides an unparalleled opportunity for emotional contact between people. This was one type of tenderness or caring that I tried to introduce into the show, for instance by selecting artists like Nicholas Cheng and Beatrice Brovia who are married to each other. I also chose Karina Nøkleby Presttun, whose stunningly-wrought embroideries are life-sized portraits of her own circle of intimate friends. This also became a way for me to address the obligation of commenting on Nordic craft: these countries have a reputation for a certain kind of care for their citizens, anchored in a concept which in Swedish is called *folkhemmet*— the idea that the government takes care of the people, that everyone is taken into consideration through a shared social contract, like a big family. This is a very particular way of thinking about politics, and one grounded in a certain tenderness, or at least humanism.

This leads me to a final point about *Tenderness*. I curated it over the period of about a year, making several visits to the Nordic region during that time. Avoiding any theoretical program other than the idea of human contact, I tended to select artists on the basis of who I actually liked. I also chose artists based on my belief that they would bring warmth and conviction to the project. It was as much about the people as about their work. It's unusual to curate with this criterion, I realize, but for this show it made sense. Among other things, the exhibition was about friends, about trust. In keeping with this, the catalogue texts I wrote were quite personal and discussed these relationships; I didn't aim for the standard critical objectivity.

Tenderness, then, was a show about generosity, vulnerability and care. It was also, of course, a show about craft. That was part of the brief.

But again, I see it as a very particular kind of craft project – and one that fell well outside the strategy of advocacy that one normally encounters. The exhibition might perhaps have seemed weak or unintellectual by art world standards. But by situating craft's ethos in family relations and other forms of implicit understanding, I hoped to escape these issues of status and focus on a more personal set of narratives.

I really enjoyed curating *Tenderness*, and at the time, I felt it might be a prototype for other exhibitions I might do in the future, at venues unknown – alongside my continuing work at the V&A. I thought I might do a series of smaller, out-of-the-way projects with an equally personal slant. Little did I know that I was about to leave London entirely, and take on a challenge of a very different kind.

Conclusion

In October 2014, I assumed the directorship at the Museum of Arts and Design in New York. One of the many changes this involved for me was a departure from curating. Now I instigate curatorial projects that are executed by others. And I must do it quickly, too. When I arrived, MAD had very little in the way of an exhibition program planned; I set to work immediately, lining up four new shows for 2014 and six for each following year. Of the 2014 shows, the most ambitious was *NYC Makers*, the first instalment of a new biennial at the museum. It was hardly a modest and personal show, as *Tenderness* was; rather, it was an attempt to position the institution as a hub for the whole creative community in New York City.

In many ways, *NYC Makers* built on the insights I'd gathered in my previous curatorial work. First, I wanted to do what I had done in *Postmodernism*, and emphasize the importance of backstage craftsmanship. New York City's economy is typically associated with finance, retail and tourism, and only rarely with manufacturing. There is even a widespread perception that New York doesn't make things at all anymore – that production has been outsourced or lost to other low-cost countries. This is a misleading caricature. Any urban fabric depends in countless ways on skilled makers; the general public may not see them, but they are there nonetheless.

The iconic moment of *NYC Makers* was a crate by the firm Boxart, which does some of the city's highest-quality packing and shipping for museums nationwide. We asked the company to make the crate for one of MAD's own collection objects, an irregular piece of sculptural furniture by the artist Wendell Castle – and then we displayed the crate with the artwork still inside, with the front taken off so that visitors could see the complicated structure of pads and props required to keep the object stable. This pointed curatorial manoeuvre had its desired effect. Boxart was recognized in the *New York Times* for its work (the company's president noted that in all the years Boxart had worked with museums, it had never before been acknowledged in an exhibition). The message about revealing processes and the necessary skills of craftspersons came through loud and clear.

Fix Fix Fix also had an echo in the show, in the form of a repaired trumpet provided by a Brooklyn-based workshop called the Brass Lab. When we invited Brass Lab's personnel to participate, they rather ingeniously bought a cheap instrument on eBay, then turned the full force of their skills on it, adding every conceivable extra feature and turning it into a top of the line horn, complete with upturned bell *a la* Dizzy Gillespie. In addition to the literal introduction of repair from the earlier project, *NYC Makers* also shared with *Fix Fix Fix* a very ecumenical approach. We included many non-art objects, and once again, they often took pride of place in the galleries (the crate is one example; others are the custom lighting, the wallpapers, a blacksmith-made mount for a velociraptor fossil, and an ecclesiastical garment made for the Catholic Church by a Jewish tailor – this is New York City, after all). In addition, we asked makers to fashion every piece of the exhibition by hand – crates, pedestals and plinths – out of unusual materials like quick-set concrete and welded steel. The overall effect was of a continuum of craftsmanship, with the objects set on a level playing field, indifferent to questions of aesthetic status.

What about *Tenderness*? Did it too have an influence on our approach to *NYC Makers*? Certainly the project was less personal for me, and it required a huge team to make it happen. In fact we tried to involve as many people as possible, from our project curator Jake Yuzna and exhibition designer Hendrik Gerrits, to the many people who nominated potential participants, to the panellists we invited to select makers for the show, to the hundred makers who finally participated (many of them were working in teams). I'd guess at least 1,000 people had a direct hand in creating the show.

Meanwhile I stayed in the director's office, raising funds for the exhibition, talking to the press, and trying to manage the execution of the show as best as I could. Yes, I did miss the direct emotion that I'd been able to find in *Tenderness*, and perhaps I'll find ways to introduce that into MAD over time. But in this initial foray, we at least reminded ourselves and others that a museum can truly draw a community into itself. On opening night, *NYC Makers* was filled with makers and their friends and families. I saw a lot of flowers being handed out. I feel confident in saying that there was a great deal of happiness, even love, in our galleries. It strikes me now, looking back, that this is the highest aspiration a museum director could hope for. And somewhere behind it all is craft, still there, still essential. Thank goodness.

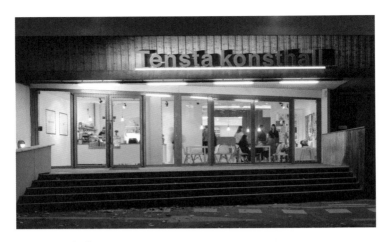

Tensta konsthall
Photo: Jean-Baptiste Beranger

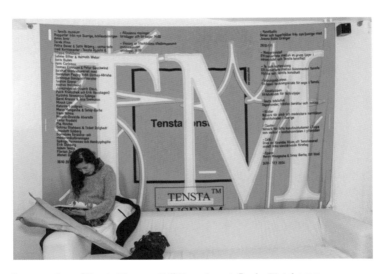

Inauguration of Tensta Museum Fall Department; flag by Metahaven
Photo: Jean-Baptiste Beranger

Tensta Museum:
Reports from New Sweden

Maria Lind

Imagine a structure that simultaneously resembles a spaceship and a ruin. It has just landed in a former storage space underneath a modest shopping mall in a late-modernist suburb of Stockholm, a part of Sweden's nation-wide Million Dwelling Programme (1965-1974). The structure is grey and angular but changes its skin constantly, since video projectors shower it with abstracted images of rectilinear spaces, darkness dotted with stars and words set in black and white against a bright pink background, the latter recognizable as the Sex Pistols' first album cover. Suddenly there is footage from a very similar structure set in a green park surrounded by blue sky. Just as with the spaceship-ruin in the former storage space, you can enter the filmed structure, and in the structure in the green park, you can even climb stairs to reach its top floor.

Artists Thomas Elovsson's and Peter Geschwind's science-fiction-inspired model *Time-Space Shuttle (Apollo Pavilion)* is a reworked version of the painter Victor Pasmore's abstract sculpture *Apollo Pavilion* (1969), which is located in the middle of a housing area in Peterlee. Peterlee is a small mining community south of Newcastle in England, and it was part of the British New Town housing project that began in the 1950s. Similar in many ways to the Swedish Million Dwelling Programme, the New Town project entailed a huge commitment to residential building. The *Apollo Pavillion* – a mix of brutalist pavilion, bridge and sculpture – had long been vandalized and despised, but a few years ago a campaign managed by a hair's breadth to save it from being razed. It has now been restored and is enjoyed by many inhabitants of Peterlee.

In the version by Elovsson and Geschwind, the pavilion is moved from its original context, redone, and placed in another context. While containing its British history, it also acquires a more speculative form that reveals what the pavilion could be in another time and place. The whole project reflects Elovsson's interest in recent art history. And as is so often the case with Geschwind, he drew inspiration from science-fiction films and computer games in making video-projections on the pavilion's exterior. Is it a UFO, a space rocket, or perhaps a ruin from the future? It attests to parallel stories and the undiscovered possibilities of a building once considered hopeless.

Time-Space Shuttle (Apollo Pavilion) was commissioned for *Tensta Museum: Reports from New Sweden* (henceforth referred to as *Tensta Museum*). This was an exhibition about history and memory in Stockholm's district of Tensta, both in relation to the place and to the people who live and work there. It took place at Tensta konsthall from October 2013 to May 2014, but it had a life before that, and an afterlife too, which still continues. In the exhibition, some 40 artists, architects, local associations, performers, sociologists, cultural geographers, philosophers and others addressed the past through artworks, research projects, seminars, symposiums and guided walks. Through these means, they also reported on the condition of Tensta today, particularly as a concrete image of what can be described as the New Sweden – a Sweden that must be understood very differently from how it was several decades ago. New Sweden is home to people with vastly different backgrounds, and it is a place where economic and social distinctions are intensifying. According to a recent report by the Organisation for Economic Cooperation and Development, of all the OECD's 34 member states, income gaps in Sweden are increasing the most rapidly. In light of this, it is worth noting that some participants who contributed to *Tensta Museum* used their works to look ahead and propose future scenarios.

Tensta is an unusually multifaceted place. Its most tangible feature is a large late-modernist housing area built between 1967 and 1972, as part of the Million Dwelling Programme. Nearly 6,000 dwellings share space with Iron Age graves, runestones, a twelfth-century church (one of the oldest buildings in the Stockholm region) with a famous Baroque chapel, and a former military training area from the early twentieth century that is now a protected nature reserve. Around 19,000 people live in Tensta today. Roughly 90 percent have a trans-national background, many from the Middle East and North Africa. This means the collective memory of Tensta is fragmented; it also means that tensions and conflicts erupt over historical and heritage-related issues. *Tensta Museum* also addressed the concept of cultural heritage

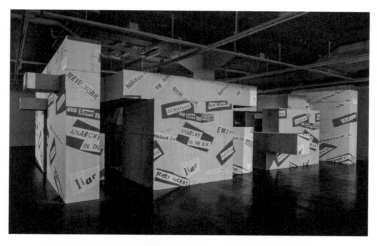

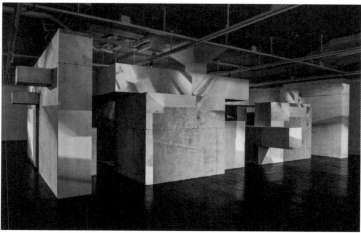

Thomas Elovsson and Peter Geschwind, *Time: Space Shuttle (Apollo Pavilion)*, 2013; model in cellophane plastic, video projection
Photo: Jean-Baptiste Beranger

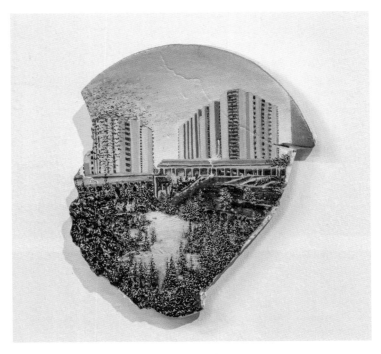

Viktor Rosdahl, *Elineberg 2020*, 2009; oil on plaster
Photo: Jean-Baptiste Beranger

and the complicated matter of how it is used in Sweden and elsewhere in Europe today. Just as the struggle for collective memory can be liberating, it can also exclude certain people and even lead to war. A preoccupation with the past is fundamentally ambivalent, yet it is impossible to deny the close bonds between a new 'respect' for history – both real and imaginary – and a sense of belonging, collective consciousness and identity promised by shared memory. With the concept of 'cultural heritage' as a thematic point of departure, *Tensta Museum* examined what it actually means when the public debate concerning memory and history is replaced by a preoccupation with memory and 'heritage'.

What, for instance, does it mean for extreme right-wing organizations and political parties – fascists in particular – to claim rights of interpretation over the idea of national heritage? The symposium *Cultural Heritage: A Treasure That Is Seeking Its Value* addressed this question. It was produced through collaboration with Stockholm City Museum and took place at Tensta konsthall on 7 March 2013, as part of the *Tensta Museum programme*. Curated by the philosopher Boris Buden (based in Zagreb and Berlin), the symposium included talks by Francoise Vergès, professor at the Center for Cultural Studies, Goldsmiths College, London, on the purpose of cultural heritage from a postcolonial perspective; Owe Ronström, professor of ethnology at the University College of Gotland, on the cultural-heritage situation in Sweden; and Eszter Babarczy, associate professor at Moholy-Nagy University of Art and Design, Budapest, on the cultural strategies of Hungary's political right wing.

The attendant programme for *Tensta Museum* offered a rich array of events throughout the seven-month exhibition period, allowing manifold interests and forms of expression to narrate the past, present and future. In the process, Tensta konsthall played the role of a museum in order to produce the authority necessary for discussing history, but also to indicate a desire for stability and continuity for the institution. It was a self-institutionalizing gesture that should be seen in light of the need of Tensta konsthall, an underfunded private foundation established in 1998, to become more stable. Since its establishment, it has in fact been run more like a project than an institution, in line with the neo-liberal 'projectification' – of everything from social work and education to cultural activities – which has been going on since the 1990s, and which by now has created a pressing need for institutional continuity in general.

The 'Tensta Museum' in the exhibition title points to far more than the institution where the exhibition was held or to the housing estate. It is in many ways much more than an exhibition or even an institution; it has developed into an organism with a life of its own, absorbing artworks, artefacts, documentary photography and other archival material. It has, among other things, become a place for doing research, for holding debates and for discussing future scenarios. For example, starting in the spring of 2012, well in advance of the exhibition opening, we held seminars every other month with a dozen people who eventually contributed to the project. They addressed the history and memory of the location as well as the notion of cultural heritage. Boris Buden functioned as the 'project philosopher', as a fellow traveller giving various kinds of input. All the seminar participants were invited to make new work or add new research to the exhibition.[1] To self-institutionalize is a well-known artistic strategy, famous examples being Marcel Duchamp and his *Boite-en-Valise*, and Marcel Broodthaers' *Museum of Modern Art, Department of Eagles*. Another is the group exhibition *The Institute of Cultural Anxiety,* held at the Institute of Contemporary Art in London in 1994. It included works by Thomas Ruff, Douglas Gordon and Claire Barclay, as well as artefacts such as meteorites and the helmet worn by Donald Campbell on his ill-fated attempt to break the water speed record. Curated by Jeremy Millar and installed in a space made to look like a generic institution with the lower parts of the walls painted green, the exhibition dealt with the anxiety that Miller deemed to surround knowledge in Western culture. More recent initiatives towards self-institutionalization are the brittle *WYSPA Institute of Contemporary Art* in Gdansk and the tiny but influential *Artists' Institute* in New York, both of which don over-sized costumes, as it were.

But to return to *Tensta Museum;* the exhibition's 'backbone' consisted of richly detailed paintings by Viktor Rosdahl, anchored in his experiences of growing up in a violent quarter of a late-modernist

---

1   In addition to the team at Tensta konsthall, the participants were Ricardo-Osvaldo Alvarado, Petra Bauer, Boris Buden, Thomas Elovsson, Barakat Gebrahwariat, Peter Geschwind, Järvaprojektet (Fredrik Ehlin, Patrik Kretschek and Erik Rosshagen), Bernd Krauss, Katarina Lundgren, Helena Mattsson, Meike Schalk, Nina Svensson and Sofia Wiberg.

housing project in a small Swedish town. Urban planning, the Million Dwelling Programme and 'the place' have long been themes in Rosdahl's art, not as a physical expression of a vanquished dream, but as a place where things happen. Other references for his art are music and the book *The Coming Insurrection* (first published in French by the Invisible Committee, 2007), which talks about a new feeling of community. The book emanates from the French counterpart to the kind of housing area that Rosdahl depicts, and it takes into account recurring social uprisings that only occasionally reach the international news. Rosdahl's paintings are examples of an under-discussed genre within contemporary art, namely, works dealing with late-modernist housing estates.

This genre was present in *Tensta Museum: Reports from New Sweden* through a 'mini-exhibition' of works reflecting late-modern housing estates. It confirmed the great interest artists have had in the subject since the 1990s. Tensta and the Million Dwelling Programme are certainly not isolated – the global phenomenon of late-modernist housing is mirrored by a global engagement with it by artists, who typically have a more complex understanding of the areas than, for example, mainstream media and politicians. Whereas the latter tend to describe the areas as dull, ugly and dangerous, the former often identify contentious points about planning processes, original ambitions and occurrences of beauty. Works by (among others) Marwa Arsanios, Sabine Bitter & Helmut Weber, Dominique Gonzalez-Foerster, Terence Gower, Heidrun Holzfeind, Marion von Osten and Florian Zeyfang instantiate the point. As part of *Tensta Museum*, public tours were given of a real late-modernist dwelling, the 'model apartment' in Tensta, situated in an ordinary block of flats (now a branch of the Stockholm City Museum). The tour entailed traveling back in time to late-1960s Tensta: the apartment is a reconstruction of the Artursson family's dwelling as it was when they moved there in 1969. The family was one of the first to move into the newly built high-rise block.

The current situation in neighbourhoods like Tensta, more precisely Husby, which is located a few kilometres away, was presented through the film *Incandescence*. The film is a reflection on the experiences that young people from Husby have of the mass-media coverage of their area, of discriminatory situations in school and of everyday life. Based on interviews that the artist Behzad Khosravi Noori and the ethnologist René León Rosales conducted during the summer of

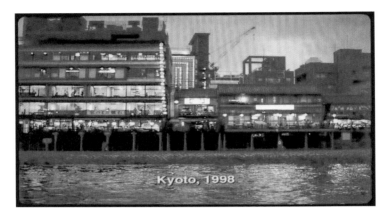

Dominique Gonzalez-Foerster, *Parc Central*, 1998–2003
Photo: Jean-Baptiste Beranger

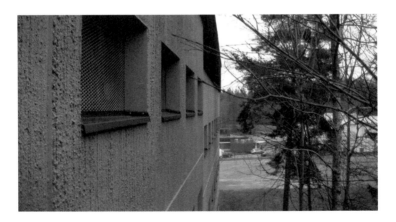

Behzad Khosravi Noori. Incandescence, 2014. Video, 51 min

2013 with young people engaged in Megafonen,[2] the film tells about an organization that works for social justice in stigmatized and economically deprived neighbourhoods.

Megafonen works with young people from such areas by offering help with homework and by organizing youth camps, seminars, demonstrations and so forth. During the so-called riots that followed the deadly shooting of a 68-year-old man during a police intervention in Husby in the spring of 2013, Megafonen was one of the voices in the debate that put the events into the context of the area's socioeconomic vulnerability. It also highlighted inaccuracies in the police's initial information about the man's death. Many cars were burned in connection with the unrest, so images of burning cars came to be what many people outside Husby associated with the area. In the film, Khosravi Noori uses Megafonen members' own testimonies of discrimination in everyday life to elucidate the exclusion that must be seen as a background to both youth engagement and to the events in Husby in 2013.

A distinctly different picture of the life of young people in the area is sketched in *BSB – Bland svarskallar och blekfisar (Pride of Race and Pride of Place)*, a documentary film from 1988 that was produced and directed by Brita Landoff, co-produced by Swedish Television. In the spring of 1988, half the students at Tensta Gymnasium (the senior high school) had a family background from Sweden, while the families of the other half came from about 30 other countries. The film shows the living organism that a school can be, with the constant movement of people and ideas. Here individuals with different reference points and experiences are placed together. What connects them is their youth and ambition to acquire a Swedish education, but the differences between them come into greater focus when we see them having to deal with perspectives other than their own. We hear some of the students' voices, like Therese from Borlänge, Alejandro from Montevideo, Aycan from Homs, Esperanza from Beirut and Suad from Tigray.

The film depicts an earlier time, before the 1990s economic crisis, but one that was still less than idyllic. The 'BSB' in the Swedish title stands for 'Bevara Sverige Blandat', which translates as 'Keep Sweden Mixed', in reaction to the then-prevalent racist slogan 'BSS' (Keep Sweden Swedish). The film tries to capture a piece of history: the energy of

2   http://megafonen.com/

91

a time that was characterized by a certain optimism – the end of the Cold War – a short period before new conflicts prompted new waves of refugees. It is a rhapsodic narrative, an attempt to catch individual stories and perspectives that are mixed up in turmoil or in the scheduled chaos that a school represents.

Since Tensta Gymnasium is an important institution in Tensta – one which represents relative continuity in a volatile neighbourhood – it became a recurring reference point in *Tensta Museum*. Tensta Gymnasium opened in 1984 and celebrated its 30th anniversary during the exhibition period. Nevertheless, its origins, via the school Norra Latin, date back to medieval Stockholm. In fact, Tensta Gymnasium could have celebrated 699 years, since the story of its administrative predecessor, the village school in Stockholm's Old Town, can be documented from the year 1315. In 1814 the school moved to Riddarholmen, and in 1890 it moved into a new grand building, Norra Latin, at Norra Bantorget. This was the start of a brilliant period in the school's history, Norra Latin being considered the best and most prestigious school in the whole country (until the 1950s it was only open to boys). In 1983/84, classes at Norra Latin were closed and transferred to Tensta. Tensta Gymnasium was meant to follow in the footsteps of its predecessor, to excel and be a model for future upper-secondary education. This aim was meant to be aided by an architecturally ambitious building designed by Gösta Uddén. What literally materializes the school's history is its art collection: it has survived all re-organizations and moves from previous locations. Four works from this collection were included in *Tensta Museum's* 'spring department' (elucidated below), [3] one being a sketch for a fresco by Carl Larsson, often considered Sweden's most well-known artist. In a seminar at Tensta konsthall, Landoff and headmistress Sofie Abrahamsson discussed Tensta Gymnasium's 30 years of operation. Also as part of *Tensta Museum*, there was an open house at the school, with Landoff's film being shown in the auditorium.

In *Tensta Museum,* old and new artworks were shown alongside other materials and artefacts. There were for instance satirical

---

3   The four works were Axel Fahlcrantz, *Riddarhomen and Söder in a Moonlit Atmosphere*, ca. 1900; Carl Larsson, *Headmaster Lundberg and Two Teachers*, 1890; Veronica Nygren, *The Hare in Autumn*, 1984; Torsten Renqvist, *The Dog, the Bird, the Boat*, 1954.

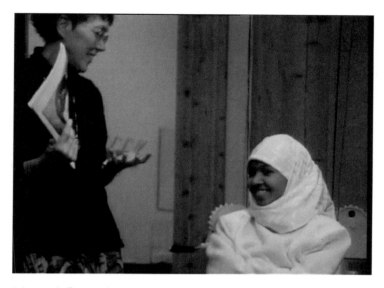

Brita Landoff, *BSB: Bland svarskallar och blekfisar (Pride of Race and Pride of Place)*, 1988; documentary, 58 min.

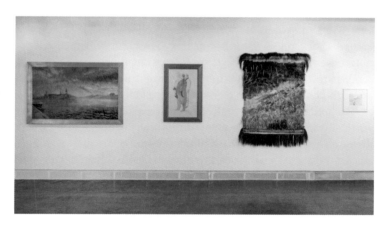

Left to the right: Axel Fahlcrantz, *Riddarholmen and Söder in a Moonlit Atmosphere*, ca 1900; Carl Larsson, *Headmaster Lundberg and Two Teachers*, 1890; Veronica Nygren, *The Hare in Autumn*, 1984; Torsten Renqvist, *The Dog, the Bird, the Boat*, 1954
Photo: Jean-Baptiste Beranger

drawings by the exiled artist Amin Amir, which addressed the political situation in Somalia. Printed out from Amir's website, which is popular within Somalia and amongst people in the diaspora, these were displayed on a bulletin board and became the starting point for a series of afternoon events co-organized with the Somali Association, the major organization for one of Tensta's largest groups. The topic for one event was 'Representations of Somalia', and the programme included the Swedish premiere of a Canadian documentary on Amir. The largest of Tensta's ethnic associations, also one of the oldest, is the Kurdish Association. It lent a selection of documents, images and publications from its archive. These were accompanied by a series of co-organized events with poetry and films from Kurdistan. Amir's drawings and the Kurdish archival material were shown alongside material on Tensta's architectural history, borrowed from architect Erik Stenberg's private archive. Previously a resident of Tensta, Stenberg has collected articles, books, catalogues and even original drawings by Tensta's planning architect, Igor Dergalin. In a number of guided walks through Tensta, Stenberg shared his deep knowledge of the history of the built environment in the neighbourhood.

'The politics of listening' is the theme of a long-term collaborative project carried out by the artist Petra Bauer, the social scientist Sofia Wiberg and the trans-ethnic association Tensta-Hjulsta Women's Center. Their project was presented in an installation and a series of 'acts' or seminars. Here questions concerning housing and housing conditions comprised one of the main threads running through several of the exhibition's projects. The showcasing of ten naïve watercolours by Josabeth Sjöberg (1812–1882) (on loan from Stockholm City Museum's collection) was an important contribution to the exhibition's subtheme on housing conditions, and a rare case of classical 'Stockholmiana' travelling to the suburbs, thereby connecting the inner city and the outskirts. As an unmarried woman with few means, Sjöberg could never afford a home of her own. She moved between various rented rooms in the Södermalm district – 'the Tensta of nineteenth-century Stockholm', with a population of workers, newly arrived migrants and others living under precarious conditions. All this Sjöberg depicted in detail in her remarkable watercolours. Also as part of the exhibition programme, the Royal Institute of Technology's architecture department and the Association of Stockholm Architects presented a series of lectures dealing with housing conditions and housing construction.

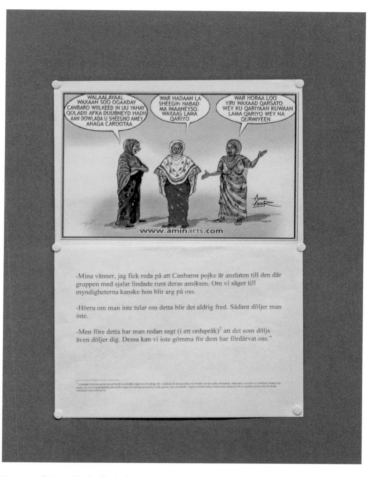

Images of Somalia, bulletin board, seminar series, workshops
Photo: Jean-Baptiste Beranger

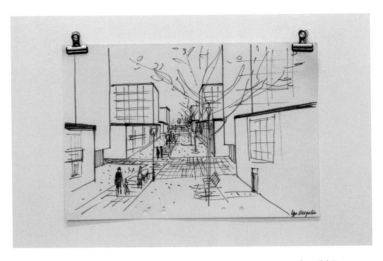

Original sketch of Tensta by the architect Igor Dergalin, as part of *Build Tensta:
A Constructed Archive*, 2013, the archive of the architect Erik Stenberg
Photo: Jean-Baptiste Beranger

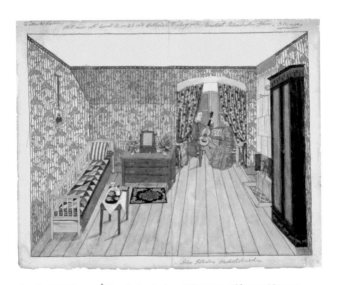

Josabeth Sjöberg, Åttonde bostaden: Mitt rum uti huset *N:ro 25
vid Cathrina Högbergsgata, Qvarteret Pelarbacken större, 3 tr upp*,
1842–46; borrowed from Stockholm City Museum

Tensta Museum did not deal exclusively with housing and late modernist architecture: the work by the art collective Järva Project focused on an often-overlooked but nevertheless important aspect of Tensta's location and topography, namely rural and suburban life. The Järva Project presented an aquarium with stone loach and a video. To make the latter, it used documentary film methods and 'gogolesque' narratives to investigate the relationship between fauna and suburbs, nature and the built environment.[4] The film concerns a rare and protected fish, the stone loach, which lives in the overgrown stream running through the nature reserve Järvafältet on the edge of Tensta. Researchers at the Swedish Museum of Natural History gave the stone loach a decisive role in city planning when they put a stop to the exploitation of the Järva fields during the building boom in the 1990s. In cooperation with the Spånga Local Heritage Society, a selection of photographs from the Society's collection was presented. Devoted to the theme of Tensta's rural heyday, most of the photos were taken prior to the start of the afore-mentioned Million Dwelling Programme. Members of the Society held several lectures on the theme of 'old Tensta' and participated in discussions on how Tensta's Million Dwelling Programme-buildings, in their view, can become part of cultural heritage. Yet another event in the programme was organized by the architect Peter Lang and the group STEALTH.unlimited.[5] Focusing on future developments, they organized a session that envisioned four scenarios for Tensta in the year 2030 – among other things, proposing a 'Tensta model' for how to deal with direct democracy.

A participatory art project that pertained to current conditions in Tensta is the *Silent University*, initiated by the artist Ahmet Ögüt at Tate Modern in 2012. The Silent University is an autonomous knowledge-exchange platform run by and for asylum seekers, refugees, and migrants who hold degrees from their home countries, but who lack the opportunity to apply their knowledge in Sweden. The project aims to expose the systematic failure to take advantage of the enormous sophistication of so many who find themselves marginalized in their new home country. As part of *Tensta Museum*, and in collaboration with Arbetarnas bildningsförbund (ABF, The Workers' Educational

---

4   http://www.erikrosshagen.se/erik/51-2/ (accessed 17 March 2015)
5   http://www.spatialagency.net/database/stealth.unlimited (accessed 9 March 2015)

Association), a series of talks was arranged in the Association's premises in the city centre. In the exhibition space itself, one could find a reference library with publications on radical pedagogy and initiatives partaking in the so-called 'educational turn' in the artworld.

Like most museums, the exhibition *Tensta Museum* had departments, but rather than having spatial or thematic parameters, these departments were based on time: the fall department and the spring department. Some works remained throughout the entire exhibition period, in the very spots where they were first installed, for instance Elovsson's and Gewschind's *Time-Space Shuttle (Apollo Pavilion)* and Rosdahl's painting *Elineberg 2020*. Others, like *The Silent University Reference Library*, were moved to a different location in the exhibition space. Yet others were part of only one department. Tensta konsthall's exhibition space is roughly 500 square meters. As a formerly unused storage space located under a shopping mall, it has a low ceiling supported by robust pillars. The floor is plywood painted glossy black – an artwork by Wade Guyton made for the 2012 exhibition *Abstract Possible: The Stockholm Synergies*. Not only did the exhibition/museum physically change over time, it also offered a dynamic viewing experience: most of the individual pieces could be seen from different angles, but at the same time they formed part of a larger entity. The soundtrack for the exhibition was set on a 30-minute loop followed by a half-hour of silence; it enveloped the whole exhibition in a subdued base rhythm that gently triggered visitors to move around. Composed by Adam Taal, known as the hip-hop celebrity Adam Tensta, the soundtrack also stimulated the movement of thoughts beyond the exhibition space as such.

This kind of spectatorship model has been described by the art historian Charlotte Klonk as 'constructivist', since it harkens back to how, in the early years of the Soviet Union, artists connected their installations to artistic contexts.[6] The constructivist spectatorship model is characterized by multiple perspectives and various possible ways of moving through an exhibition space. The artworks are not meant to be seen by one isolated person at a time, but by people who share in a collective viewing experience. Klonk argues that this differs from the model prevalent in the nineteenth century, as expressed in

---

6   Charlotte Klonk, *Spaces of Experience* (London: Yale University Press, 2009).

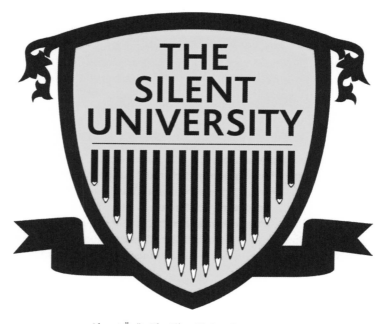

Ahmet Ögüt, The Silent University, 2013–2014

national art museums in Paris, Berlin and London, where the set-up was geared towards educating the audience person by person, through more or less static presentations. She calls this the 'educated spectatorship model', the purpose being to educate visitors to become good citizens. The constructivist spectatorship model also deviates from the consumptionist model pioneered by the Museum of Modern Art in New York. Here the installation has a clear beginning and end, offering one work for viewing at a time. Sometimes the objects on view could even be purchased in the museum store. In this way, a 'good consumer' is being trained. Whereas both the citizen and the consumer models are essentially didactic in more or less outspoken ways, the constructivist model is primarily based on more abstract and atmospheric experiences.

The constructivist spectatorship model has been employed in other places and at other times as well, but mostly unbeknownst to the artists and curators using it. More often than not, such exhibitions are collaborative and atmospheric. Examples are the research-based exhibitions at the Shedhalle in Zurich in the 1990s, which were curated by (among others) Renate Lorenz and Ursula Biemann. Other examples are the visceral and yet abstract exhibitions of Dominique Gonzalez-Foerster, Pierre Huyghe and Philippe Parreno from around the same time. A number of exhibitions I have worked on since the mid-1990s share some of these features and concerns. Starting in 1979, the collective Group Material, based in New York, had a similarly conscious take on the exhibition as a format and artistic medium in its own right, since the group often installed works in ways that made the viewing experience dynamic. Group Material's first exhibition, which was held in the group's storefront space in the East Village, was entitled *The People's Choice;* it consisted of objects submitted by the neighbours under the rubric of 'my favourite object'. The event called 'Salon Tensta' in *Tensta Museum's* fall department, offered a similar opportunity to neighbours. An open invitation was sent out to the community, to submit words, sounds and images related to Tensta. From the material that was sent in, a selection was made by, among others, the hip-hop artist Adam Tensta, and Maria Lantz, photographer and rector of the University College of Arts, Crafts and Design, Stockholm. The salon thus became a mini-exhibition within the exhibition.

Like any museum with ambitions, *Tensta Museum* also had branches: one at Stockholm City Museum and a second at the Museum of Medieval Stockholm. At Stockholm City Museum, the artist Katarina Lundgren presented a new work based on Granholmstoppen, a man-made hill composed of materials removed from Tensta when the housing estate was built at Järva Field. At the Museum of Medieval Stockholm, the artists Bernd Krauss and Nina Svensson presented the *Tensta Horse Racing Society*, a work harkening back to the time when horses from the nearby horse-racing track Solvalla spent their summers on the farms of old Tensta. This work recalled a popular pastime that is virtually absent from the sphere of culture.

Part of *Tensta Museum* even went on tour: *Tensta Museum on the Move* travelled to the curatorial collective WHW's space Galerija Nova in Zagreb. Another part, which was accessible to anyone with an internet connection, was Tensta-based Meron Mangasha and Senhay Berhe's *Blue Blood*, a tribute to an underground train in words and moving images.[7] Other projects took place at Tensta Gymnasium and in the library in Tensta, where Hans Carlsson's art project *Artoteket* enabled people to borrow newly-commissioned art using a library card. In addition to this, *Tensta Museum* hosted historical walks and seminars with people who had experienced early Tensta. The cultural geographer Irene Molina lectured on the increasing ethnic and socioeconomic segregation visible in Tensta and other Million Dwelling Programme areas. While Tensta library was being renovated during winter 2013 and spring 2014, Tensta konsthall was asked to act as a branch library. Thus some library books, especially children's books and books on local history, were available during the exhibition period.[8]

Another way of looking at *Tensta Museum* is as a 'contact zone'.[9] The anthropologist Mary Louise Pratt uses this term to describe social spaces where various cultures collide and try to deal with each other, often through asymmetrical relations of power. The contexts Pratt refers to tend to involve colonialism, slavery and their repercussions.

---

7   It was viewable at www.tenstakonsthall.se/space, but is no longer accessible.
8   Four texts specially written for *Tensta Museum* could be found online at www. tenstakonsthall.se/bag: 'Historien om Tensta konsthall' (The Story of Tensta konsthall) by Jan Ekman, 'Tensta – en plats som ständigt ska bli batter' (Tensta – A Place That Is Constantly Going to Be Better) by Emma Holmqvist, 'Mamsell Josabeth Sjöberg' by Lawen Mohtadi, and 'Kulturarv' (Cultural Heritage) by Boris Buden.
9   Mary Louise Pratt: Arts of the Contact Zone, *Profession* (New York: Modern Language Association, 1991), pp. 33-40.

She also uses the term to reconsider the community models that feature in academia and social work. Seen as a contact zone, *Tensta Museum* includes a certain amount of 'autoethnographic' material, that is, texts, images and other documents in which people describe themselves. In this material, they also deal with the representations that others make of them, as well as with material produced by people who do not live and work in Tensta. This is a form of 'transculturation' whereby subordinate groups engage with material from a dominant group, replacing reductive concepts of assimilation that are common in characterizations of colonial cultures. Many projects within *Tensta Museum* testify to the fact that subordinate groups cannot usually control what comes out of the dominant culture, but it is possible – and usual – to determine what gets absorbed and how.

While a contact zone in Pratt's understanding is primarily spatial, *Tensta Museum* also evoked it on the level of time, as for instance in the *Aktion Arkiv Tensta* project. To explain this it is necessary to back up a bit: In 1989, Stockholm's *fastighetsnämnd* (property committee) organized a large international housing conference in Tensta, with invited experts from important renewal projects in, for example, France, Turkey, the United Kingdom and the United States. The conference became the starting point for a new era of citizen participation and housing renewal projects that were carried out through collaboration with residents. Most of the material from the conference had been lost, possibly because of reorganization within the local authority, possibly because of lack of interest. The architects and researchers Helena Mattsson, Meike Schalk and Sara Brolund de Carvalho, however, contend that the conference and the subsequent renewal projects are central to Swedish history and crucial for understanding the development of architecture and the urban history of Tensta.

In *Tensta Museum's* spring department, therefore, Mattsson, Schalk and Brolund de Carvalho used *Aktion Arkiv Tensta* to create an interactive and mobile archive. The wooden construction was mounted on a set of wheels and built to fit in the elevators of Stockholm's subway system. It could be moved swiftly to any place that needed an 'activist archive' for collecting undocumented knowledge and material on the verge of disappearing. The archive changed during the exhibition period, partly through changes in the collected material and partly through focusing on three different themes. First, the housing renewal conference in 1989 was the centre of attention, followed by Cooperative Project Tensta (1989-95 at Glömmingegränd by Loggia architects AB and the architect Ylva Larsson) and finally, citizens' initiatives from the 1960s and '70s up to the present. These three themes were actualized through a witness seminar on the housing renewal conference in 1989, with conference participants such as architect Rod Hackney and planner Erol Sayin; a seminar at Glömmingegränd with, among others, Ylva Larsson; and a debate called 'The Battle for Space', with invited activists from the 1960s to today.

Tensta Museum: Reports from New Sweden officially closed in May 2014. Nevertheless, the debates, negotiations and struggles over questions such as 'Whose history is at stake here?', 'How about the present?' and 'What kind of future do we want to create?' are very much alive. The organism is kicking, the contact zones are active. *Time-Space Shuttle (Apollo Pavilion)* and the projection with words set in black and white against a bright pink background testify to the fact that things can be different. And they surely will be. Today the once-hated and dilapidated Apollo Pavilion is renovated and declared an official English Heritage site. And the Sex Pistols, the quintessential subcultural phenomenon whose first album cover was pink with the black and white words, have been recommended to receive the same status.

Contributors

André Gali is editor-in-chief of *Norwegian Crafts Magazine* and series-editor of *Documents on Contemporary Crafts*. He is also founding editor of the Nordic art quarterly *Kunstforum* and the website www. kunstforum.as, founded in 2009. Gali holds a Master's degree in theatre theory with a thesis entitled 'Andy Warhol Superstar: On the Artist Myth, Media and Mechanical Theatricality' (2005). As a freelance art critic, photographer, essayist, journalist and lecturer, Gali has published essays on art and economy, queer and feminist art practices, the gaze of the middle class, and contemporary art jewellery. Recent catalogues and books he has contributed to are *Reinhold Ziegler: Cosmic Debris* (Arnoldsche Art Publishers, 2014), *Aftermath of Art Jewellery* (Arnoldsche Art Publishers, 2013), *Museum for Skills* (editor, Norwegian Crafts, 2013), *Morten Andenæs: Skyldfolk* (Teknisk Industri, 2012), *Never Mind the Benefits* (Feil Forlag, 2012) and *Sigurd Bronger: Laboratorium Mechanum* (Arnoldsche Art Publishers, 2011). Gali has been on the board of the Norwegian Critic's Association (2009-2011) and leader of the art section at the Norwegian Critic's Association (2010-2012).

CURATORS

Glenn Adamson is the director of the Museum of Arts and Design (MAD) in New York. He was previously head of research at the Victoria & Albert Museum (V&A) in London, where he helped initiate and shape major exhibitions, managed partnerships with museums and universities, and led academic fundraising. Adamson also contributed to the V&A's publications, educational programming, media relations and commercial activities. During his tenure at the V&A, in addition to work in the Research Department, Adamson also curated modern and contemporary design exhibitions. Worth special mention are his co-curations of the major survey exhibition *Postmodernism: Style and Subversion 1970 to 1990* (opened in 2011 in London and travelled on to Italy and Switzerland), and the forthcoming exhibition *The Future: A History*, which will inaugurate the V&A's new temporary exhibition galleries in 2017. Adamson has published several books including *The Invention of Craft* (V&A, Bloomsbury, 2013), *The Craft Reader* (Berg, 2010) and *Thinking Through Craft* (V&A, Berg, 2007). He is founding co-editor of the *Journal of Modern Craft*, a peer-reviewed academic journal. Prior to his work at the V&A, from 2000 to 2005, Adamson served as curator for the Chipstone Foundation in Milwaukee, Wisconsin, which collects and promotes research within the field of decorative arts. During that period, Adamson was responsible for organizing exhibitions, consulting on acquisitions, and development. He also served as adjunct curator at the Milwaukee Art Museum, where he organized a number of exhibitions, including the award-winning *Industrial Strength Design: How Brooks Stevens Shaped Your World* (2003). Born and raised in Boston, Adamson received his BA in art history from Cornell University (1994) and earned his doctorate in art history from Yale University (2001). He serves as chairman of the board of trustees for the Crafts Study Centre, Farnham, and is the most recent recipient of the mid-career Iris Award for outstanding contributions to the decorative arts.

Maria Lind is a curator and writer based in Stockholm. Currently she is the director of Tensta konsthall, Stockholm.

Marianne Zamecznik is a free-lance curator and exhibition designer based in Berlin. From 2007 to 2010 she served as program director at 0047, an independent Oslo-based organization for projects in and in between the fields of art and architecture. Focusing mainly on exhibition making, her practice overlaps the fields of art, design and craft. She is a guest lecturer at Oslo National Academy of the Arts and an artistic consultant for KORO, Public Art Norway. Recent projects include *Der Dilettant* at LYNX 760, Oslo (solo); *The End of the Night* at LACE, Los Angeles; *La Fin de La Nuit* at Palais de Tokyo, Paris (exhibition design for curator Martha Kirszenbaum); *Form against Background* at Atopia, Oslo (curator); *Revealing Thoughts* at Revelations, Grand Palais, Paris (exhibition design); *Rosa Tannenzapfen – Choreography of Species*, which was a project co-curated with Elena Tzotzig for Paolo Chiasera's project *Exhibition Painting* at the 7th Momentum biennial; *The Running Room* at Space for Art and Industry, New York (co-curated with Anders Smebye); *The Feast* at the European Culture Congress, Wroclaw, Poland (curator); *Imagine Being Here Now*, the 6th

Momentum biennial, Moss, Norway (part of the curatorial team and exhibition design with Øystein Aasan); and *The Space Between Us* at The Modern Museum of Warsaw (curator). She is currently co-editing a book about exhibition architecture with Carson Chan. Zamecznik studied at Oslo National Academy of the Arts and at the University College of Arts, Crafts and Design in Stockholm.

Anne Britt Ylvisåker holds a *Cand. Philol.* degree in art history from the University of Bergen. She works as senior curator at KODE - Art Museums of Bergen, where she has chief responsibility for contemporary craft, textiles and ceramics. She has been responsible for numerous projects at the museum, including *Brennpunkt Bergen – keramikk 1950-2000* (Burning Point Bergen – Ceramics 1950 – 2000) and *Strikk 7* (Knit 7). From 2008-2011 she participated in the research group *Creating Artistic Value – A Research Project on Rubbish and Readymades, Art and Ceramics,* funded by the Research Council of Norway. She taught art history at the Norwegian National College of Craft and Design (Statens Høgskole for Kunsthåndverk og Design) (1988-1996) and was director of Sogn Folk Museum (1992-1994). She has written various books and articles on handicrafts, craft and visual art, such as *Husflid*, *Farge i målarkunsten*, *Opplegg på gang,* and *Assigning Cultural Value: Digitizing the Value – Valuing the Digitized.*

Documents on Contemporary Crafts, No 3
Crafting Exhibitions

Editor for No. 3: Crafting Exhibitions: André Gali
Senior editor of Documents on Contemporary Crafts: André Gali

Contributors: Glenn Adamson, Maria Lind, Marianne Zamecznik and
Anne Britt Ylvisåker
Translation, proofreading: Arlyne Moi
All texts © Norwegian Crafts and the authors

Publication design: Aslak Gurholt (Yokoland)
Typeset in Tiempos Text 8.5/12.5
Printed on Munken Pure 120g, Arctic Paper, Sweden
Printed by Nilz & Otto Grafisk AS, Norway

Bibliographic information published by the Deutsche Nationalbibliothek
The Deutsche Nationalbibliothek lists this publication in the Deutsche
Nationalbibliografie; detailed bibliographic data are available on the Internet at
www.dnb.de.

ISBN 978-3-89790-429-3

Published by
Norwegian Crafts
Rådhusgaten 20, 0151 Oslo, Norway
Phone: (+47) 22 91 02 60
Email: post@norwegiancrafts.no
www.norwegiancrafts.no

Arnoldsche Art Publishers
Olgastraße 137, 70180 Stuttgart, Germany
Phone +49 (0) 711 64 56 18–0
Fax +49 (0) 711 64 56 18–79
Email art@arnoldsche.com
www.arnoldsche.com

434340